CAMBRIDGE LIBRARY COLLECTION

Books of enduring scholarly value

Polar Exploration

This series includes accounts, by eye-witnesses and contemporaries, of early expeditions to the Arctic and the Antarctic. Huge resources were invested in such endeavours, particularly the search for the North-West Passage, which, if successful, promised enormous strategic and commercial rewards. Cartographers and scientists travelled with many of the expeditions, and their work made important contributions to earth sciences, climatology, botany and zoology. They also brought back anthropological information about the indigenous peoples of the Arctic region and the southern fringes of the American continent. The series further includes dramatic and poignant accounts of the harsh realities of working in extreme conditions and utter isolation in bygone centuries.

The Arctic North-East and West Passage

This short work contains texts and maps relating to early exploration and trade routes. Included here are descriptions of Russia and Siberia by Isaac Massa (1586–1643), a Dutch merchant and diplomat; one of the memorials relating to Pacific discoveries by the Portuguese explorer Pedro Fernandes de Queirós (*c*.1565–1615); and maps by the cartographer Hessel Gerritsz (*c*.1581–1632) showing the discoveries of the English navigator Henry Hudson (d.1611). Gerritsz originally compiled these materials and published them in Dutch, and they were soon translated into Latin to increase their readership. In the present work, first published in 1878, reproductions of the Dutch and Latin editions from 1612 and 1613 are presented together by Frederik Muller (1817–81). Muller also included an explanatory essay by his son Samuel Muller (1848–1922), and a new English translation.

Cambridge University Press has long been a pioneer in the reissuing of out-of-print titles from its own backlist, producing digital reprints of books that are still sought after by scholars and students but could not be reprinted economically using traditional technology. The Cambridge Library Collection extends this activity to a wider range of books which are still of importance to researchers and professionals, either for the source material they contain, or as landmarks in the history of their academic discipline.

Drawing from the world-renowned collections in the Cambridge University Library and other partner libraries, and guided by the advice of experts in each subject area, Cambridge University Press is using state-of-the-art scanning machines in its own Printing House to capture the content of each book selected for inclusion. The files are processed to give a consistently clear, crisp image, and the books finished to the high quality standard for which the Press is recognised around the world. The latest print-on-demand technology ensures that the books will remain available indefinitely, and that orders for single or multiple copies can quickly be supplied.

The Cambridge Library Collection brings back to life books of enduring scholarly value (including out-of-copyright works originally issued by other publishers) across a wide range of disciplines in the humanities and social sciences and in science and technology.

The Arctic North-East and West Passage

*Detectio Freti Hudsoni,
or Hessel Gerritsz's Collection of Tracts
by Himself, Massa and De Quir
on the N.E. and W. Passage,
Siberia and Australia*

HESSEL GERRITSZ
TRANSLATED BY FRED. JOHN MILLARD

CAMBRIDGE
UNIVERSITY PRESS

CAMBRIDGE
UNIVERSITY PRESS

University Printing House, Cambridge, CB2 8BS, United Kingdom

Cambridge University Press is part of the University of Cambridge.
It furthers the University's mission by disseminating knowledge in the pursuit of
education, learning and research at the highest international levels of excellence.

www.cambridge.org
Information on this title: www.cambridge.org/9781108075138

© in this compilation Cambridge University Press 2015

This edition first published 1878
This digitally printed version 2015

ISBN 978-1-108-07513-8 Paperback

The Arctic North-East and West Passage.

DETECTIO FRETI HUDSONI

OR

HESSEL GERRITSZ'S COLLECTION OF TRACTS

BY HIMSELF, MASSA AND DE QUIR

ON THE N. E. AND W. PASSAGE, SIBERIA AND AUSTRALIA

Reproduced, with the Maps, in *Photolithography*
in Dutch and Latin after the editions of 1612 and 1613.

AUGMENTED WITH A NEW ENGLISH TRANSLATION
by FRED. JOHN MILLARD,
English Translator at Amsterdam.

AND AN ESSAY ON THE ORIGIN AND DESIGN OF THIS COLLECTION
by S. MULLER Fz.
Keeper of the Records at Utrecht.

AMSTERDAM.
FREDERIK MULLER & Co.
1878.

Gedrukt bij Joh. Enschedé & Zonen, te Haarlem.

PREFACE.

The collection of tracts on Arctic discoveries by Hudson and the other Explorers, edited by Hessel Gerritsz. in 1612, has been often reprinted both in Dutch and in Latin. These texts, however, which present important variations, have not hitherto been printed together; nor in any edition have all the maps been given.

As this collection has been, and always will be, the principal source of our knowledge about these important researches, I have considered it advisable in the interest of science, to reproduce the very rare Dutch original; the Latin translation, and all the maps, thus utilising my good fortune as possessor of both editions.

A quite new and extremely careful translation into English has been added, the old one in the rare collection of Purchas, 1625, being incomplete, incorrect, and difficult to obtain.

As the various tracts in the book of Hessel Gerritsz have at first sight but slight internal connection, and as the idea of their combination and publication may be to many mind obscure, I have entreated Mr. S. Muller to explain the origin and design of the collection. Being the author of the „History of the Dutch Northern Company" he indeed, is the most competent authority upon the subject.

AMSTERDAM, June 1878.   FREDERIK MULLER. .

INTRODUCTION.

The little book we now beg to present to the public in its original form, is not only one of the rarest, but one of the most remarkable productions of the very fertile Netherland press in the beginning of the 17th century. However small and unassuming in appearance, it was not only the first publication issued concerning Hudsons most famous voyage, but contains also every thing we know of the plans of that great mariner. Mr. Murphy's clever essay indeed already directed the attention of the public to this side of the book. In it, and in Dr. Ashers learned disquisition concerning Hudson, the reader will find a detailed account respecting the great importance of what is here related from very good sources about Hudsons voyage, and of the maſs which accompanies this description. Only this would be sufficient to justify a reprint of this little book, of which only three or four copies are known to exist. And more than this. Besides the accounts of Hudsons

voyage,

voyage, we here find a very extensive description of the oldest commercial connexions of Russia with the then so very mysterious Siberia; we also meet with a relation of the conquest of that country, which followed shortly after, an event which is so very imperfectly known, and finally a vast treasure of most interesting particulars in a geographical point of view respecting the north of Russia and Siberia, the coast of the Ice-sea, the trading-roads in use towards the close of the 16th century, and the customs and manners of the tribes residing there. And all this we have from the hand of an eye-witness, who was a man of a cultivated taste and had come to Russia with the definite object in view of obtaining a knowledge of the country and its traffic, — who did not even hesitate to expose his life to wrest this map from the hands of the mysterious Russians. Finally this varied collection contains a remarkable, though little noticed account, from the hand of the traveller himself, concerning an expedition for the discovery of the unknown south country undertaken by the famous Pedro Fernandez de Quiros, of whom Mr. Major recently testified, that: »he left behind him a name which for merit though not for success was second only to that of Columbus."

And how the favourable opinion we have of this remarkable collection increases, when we learn that the publisher was no other than the cartographer Hessel Gerritsz., a name which perfectly warrants the

the reliability of the accounts given. Hessel Gerritsz., born in the Dutch village of Assum, belongs to the race of learned cartographers and printers, of whom the Netherland Republic was so justly proud. Well acquainted with such men as Plancius and Massa, Gerritsz. was, like his contemporaries Hondius and Blaeu, exactly the person fit to pronounce his verdict in the learned questions which are discussed in the little book he published. The fruits of his labour, among which stands foremost the little work here reprinted, testifies to his skill. We find of him moreover maps of Russia, Lithuania and other lands in the large atlass of Blaeu, — of America in the well-known work of De Laet, — of Spitsbergen and Novaya Zemlya in his own »Histoire du pays nommé Spits-bergen." There exist also maps drawn by him of Batavia, of the Indian Archipelago and even of New-Guinea. His varied knowledge already attracted the attention of the East India Company, who appointed him in 1617 their cartographer, a position which he occupied till his death, which took place in the first days of 1634. It was of course to be expected that a man of such a stamp, as soon as he published a work of this character, on a ground where he felt himself quite at home, would produce something not only perfectly answering to the exigencies of the moment, but which might be likewise of great value in our own time to historical researches. And this is most especially the case with his first known publication
entitled

entilled: »Description of the land of the Samoyeds." That his work suited the taste of his contemporaries is not only evident from the four editions it passed through, but more especially from the innumerable versions it underwent in different languages, in nearly all the geographical works of the time. We shall soon perceive on a closer survey, that the book is likewise of great importance to ourselves. We beg however first to premise a few words about the time in which it appeared, and the particular object of its publication.

The year 1612 was cast in the very centre of a period, when the general interest felt in polar navigation was at its full zenith. The East India Company, that had been called into existence by the States General, ten years ago, was now in her prime. The treasures it imported from the East Indies, a region with which one was so very imperfectly acquainted, had gradually excited the envy of the excluded Hollanders and inhabitants of Zealand. Besides this, the aversion peculiarly felt by this nation to all kinds of monopoly must be taken into account, so that soon after the erection of the Company, enterprising merchants looked round in search of means to compete with their rival. And the danger impending over the East India navigation was not a little increased, when the Twelve years Truce had deprived the vast numbers of seamen and adventurers, with whom the mariners provinces swarmed, of a fair opportunity of giving full scope to their

their wish to share the dangers and profits of long voyages and perilous battles. Also for them the remote provinces of the southern hemisphere were the only places where they could find the means of subsistence and at the same time deal the hated king of Spain, notwithstanding the Treaty, a rude blow. It is therefore at the commencement of the Treaty (1609) we perceive the efforts to vie with the East India Company assume their full vigour. Another circumstance however, likewise contributed to this state of things.

Earlier efforts, made by the enemies to the Company, had constantly proved futile from the impossibility of making an infraction on the charter of the Company; but during the last years before 1609 the general attention had again been directed to a vulnerable point, which this charter offered to the aggressors. It is a fact widely known, that the Netherlanders, who in the path of commerce and navigation generally followed with extraordinary boldness the tracks which the English had opened, had already towards the end of the 16th century also commenced the expeditions in the Ice-sea, first undertaken by their rivals. Olivier Brunel, a Netherlander, who had acquired a large fund of experience in Russian service, made the first trials; some years after followed the three world-renowned voyages of Linschoten and Barendsz., whereupon the Netherlanders, — again according to their wont, — left their English predecessors far behind them.

them. Since that time however, the misery endured
by Heemskerck and Barendsz. on their third voyage,
had intimidated their fellow countrymen from making
similar vain attempts as they were then thougth to be.
The English had likewise long given up trying to find
that way; but after some fruitless expeditions to the
north-west Henry Hudson had again drawn the public
attention to the Ice-Sea. His two voyages, undertaken
in 1607 and 1608 to Spitzbergen and Novaya Zemlya,
had again given birth to new hopes to find out the
passage, and the report of his expeditions had also
penetrated as far as the Netherlands. Immediately the
competitors of the East India Company were ready
to try this chance. The Company's license was
only available for two roads: the one round the
Cape of Good Hope, the other through the Strait of
Magellan. If a third way was found out, a fair opportunity for competition would be opened. The Company
and her enemies both resolved upon seeking out that
one. In 1609 two expeditions sailed out from the Netherland harbours towards the North. The East India
Company sent Hudson, and the wellknown Isaac le
Maire took in his service a sea-captain renowned for
his boldness Melchior van Kerckhoven. Both vessels
took a too easterly direction and struck upon the masses
of ice, which encircle Novaya Zemlya and the Strait
of Nassau. But the unlucky issue did not intimidate
the Netherlanders. Hudsons plans were again stu-
died and his proposal was hailed with avidity, to
endeavour

endeavour according to the plans already laid down by a certain Robert Thorne in 1527, to sail straight accross the pole through the open Polar-sea to East India. As early as 1611, a new expedition for the execution of this plan was ready at the expense of the Amsterdam Admiralty: Jan Cornelisz. May again sailed to the north. He neither succeeded this year nor the following in finding a passage, but this unhappy issue did not in the least diminish the zeal of the Netherlanders, witness the voyages of Pieter Fransz. to the north-west (1613), of Jan Jacobsz. May straight on to the north (1614), of the well known cartographer Mr. Joris Carolus, as mate on a vessel of the North Company to the Strait of Davis (1615) and of Wybe Jansz. again to the north-west (1616). Also in England, it was exactly at this time the searching of a passage was again zealously undertaken. In 1610 Hudson had commenced his last voyage; in 1612 two expeditions, one under Button and another under Hall, were again set afloat, and in 1615 and 1616 Bylot and Baffin performed their world-renowned voyages.

It is indeed no surprising matter, that at a time when expeditions for the discovery of the northern passage, formed the general topic of the day, the public opinion was highly interested in favour of this plan. A violent dispute was kept up among learned men concerning the plausibility of the several plans. The one would, just like Linschoten, follow the line of the

the Russian coast and hoped, through the Strait of Nassau, to get into a sea free of ice; another gave the preference to the plans of Hudson, who boasted a good deal of all he knew about an open polar sea; a third recommended, not without hesitation, the hither-to unfrequented north-west, as the place where it was most likely an ice-free passage might be found. Hessel Gerritsz. judged it necessary to enlighten his countrymen upon this subject. From his rich experience he wished to communicate, what the expeditions of the last years had brought to light concerning the relative superiority of the three plans. But as a professional nautical man, he did not at the same time wish to conceal the circumstance that he for himself felt only sanguine with respect to the north-west passage. The plans of Linschoten might perhaps still hold out a slender chance of success; but the opinion, entertained by so many, that the way round the Pole was the best, — an opinion which was again held up to notice in 1610 by a pamphlet issued by a certain Dr. Röslin, — he considered to be a mere fancy of the brain. Thorne might, in 1527, still have fostered similar adventurous plans, the voyages of Barendsz. and Hudson had, according to Gerritsz., sufficiently proved the folly of expecting any favourable result from that passage. It is even not unlikely that Plancius too, who in the supposition that Novaya Zemlya's north-eastern point was joined to the Russian conti-nent, had just like Barendsz. zealously recommended

the

the sailing round that island, — like his friend
Gerritsz., at that time despaired of the practicability
of his old plan. At all events it is certain, that both
Plancius and Gerritsz. expected much from the new
road, which Hudson, after the frustration of his first
plan, had pursued, — in the search of which Davis
had already, in 1580, reaped many a laurel and on
which Hudson himself had placed many an important step onward: the passage in the north-west. This
opinion was to find more and more adherents among
the public, and with this object Gerritsz. published
in 1612, the little work now reprinted and placed
behind this. Two particulars were, of course, to be
discussed in it: the little chance of success the way
by the north-east offered, and the great advantages
which the discovery of the north-west passage promised to the discoverers. Concerning the practicability
of this plan, it was necessary to state at the same
time, what the most recent voyages had brought to
light in this respect.

Gerritsz. himself undertook to recommend the north-
western passage; for the obtaining of information
concerning the north-eastern road he applied to his
countryman Isaac Massa, who, by the rich store of
knowledge he had amassed in Russia itself, had come
to the same conclusion Hessel Gerritsz. had.

The name of Isaac Massa is, as many others we
have just mentioned, only but recently placed in the
honourable light it deserves. In 1864, a short bio-

graphical

graphical sketch of his life appeared, which clearly points out the many claims he has to the gratitude of posterity. Isaac Massa, born at Haarlem in 1587, was sent, about 1600, to Russia to acquire a knowledge of business there. During a residence of eight years he obtained an extensive knowledge of that empire, at that time nearly quite unknown. That he, subsequently, availed himself of that knowledge, for the forming of commercial relations between his native country and the land in which he sojourned, — that he afterwards resided for a series of years, as an agent of the States-General at Moscou, — that his economical merits were by no means of an inferior kind, are particulars which it would be out of place here to dwell upon. Our attention is now rather more especially directed to Massa's great merit in having supplied us with works, which are nearly the only source from which we derive the knowledge of Rus_sia's geographical and social position, during the first years of the 17th century. Massa himself already saw the great importance, which the reports collected by him concerning Russia's northern coast and Siberia, — but only just conquered by the Czars —, might have for the discovery of the north passage to East-India, so ardently hoped for.

He had already, previous to the year 1612, expressed his desire to Prince Maurice, that he might be of some service to his country, as Heemskerk and others had already been;" he had even carried on negotiations

negotiations with Isaac Le Maire, concerning a plan to accompany the expedition himself on the vessel, fitted out by Le Maire, and which was undertaken by Van Kerckhoven with so unhappy a result. But both plans proved equally fallacious. Massa, who believed that the south part of Novaya Zemlya, which was only known to him, was nothing else than the farthest advancing point of America's northern coast, expected, of course, only something good from enterprises, which, in conformity with the first Netherland north-polar voyages, followed the line of the Russian coast, and endeavoured to reach the far east through the strait of Nassau. The difficulties, connected with that voyage, were too well known to him, from personal observation, not to advise undertaking the expedition only with the greatest caution and after long preparation. Taught by the experience of the Russians, he soon considered it indispensable to pass the winter in the north; while, at the same time, he even then conscientiously desisted from holding out any promises, as to the successful issue of the voyage. That part of the coast which was situated beyond the Ob was unknown to him, and he even not without reason doubted, whether that more remote part would offer any passage at all to East-India. It was therefore a matter of course, that the negotiations with Massa about a north-polar expedition led to no result; but, on the other hand, he was the very man, who could be of great service to

Hessel

Hessel Gerritsz. He did not believe in the possibility of finding the passage to the north of Novaya Zemlya; nor expected great results from voyages undertaken according to the plans of Linschoten; and thought nothing more desirable than to have his views on the subject made widely known.

Massa had already, during his stay in Russia, with great difficulty obtained possession of a map of the coast of the Ice-Sea from some one who had himself been in Siberia, on which was pointed out the coast of the Ice-Sea, and which had probably been drawn between 1604 and 1608 at Moscow. This map was, in 1609, provided by him with Dutch names, and he had added from some Russian annotations an account of every thing that could be communicated concerning the places delineated in it. In two little works entitled: »Description of the lands of Siberia, Samoyeda and Tingoesa," and: »A short account of the ways and rivers from Muscovy eastwards and north-eastwards by land," he had related what he knew of the first commercial relations of the Russians with Siberia and the conquest of that land which soon followed. At the same time, he had noted down the ways in which the Russians had obtained their aim, and what was the condition of the lands they had visited.

That the cartographer Hessel Gerritsz. was the right man, immediately to see the importance of these two compositions, needs no demonstration. He had no sooner become acquainted with their existence, when

when he immediately set to work, augmented what
Massa had collected with a few additional notes and had
this printed. He then added a map of the discoveries
of Hudson in the north-west, which he had composed
after an English original copy. He augmented the
same with a short relation of the expeditions of the
traveller, which he borrowed from the accounts of
Plancius. Finally, a short account of the able voyager,
Pedro Fernandez De Quiros, was added, in which
the latter largely commented on the wonders of a
country discovered by him, which was generally believed to be the long sought-for, but as yet unknown
southern continent, and which seemed to be easily
accessible along the road discovered by Hudson,
even since the way through the strait of Magellan
was closed to competitors of the East-India Company.
Hessel Gerritsz. himself wrote a short introduction,
in which he gave a short survey of the origin of the
relations of the Netherlanders with Russia, and the
far off north-easterly countries, and of the expeditions
already made for the discovery of the northern passage.

So the little book, which thus made its appearance
at the commencement of 1612, consists of several
parts which, at first sight, seem to bear but little
relation to each other, but, on a closer inspection,
severally appear to have only one object in view: that
of recommending the finding out of a northern passage,
and more particularly one in the direction approved
of by Hessel Gerritsz. We find in this collection:

1. Introduction

We beg to add a word or two on each of these works in particular.

The introduction sketches in broad outlines how Europe first became acquainted with Russia by Her bersteyn's work, — how the trade of the Netherlanders with Russia was established since, by Olivier Brunel; and how that establishment gradually enticed them further, and induced them, again in the footsteps of Brunel, to engage in enterprises to East-India, which have rendered Linschoten's and Barentsz.' memory immortal. The inference drawn from these several facts is, that the finding of a passage in this direction,

direction is improbable, and with vehemence Gerritsz.
then attacks the plans which gave rise to the voyage
of Jan Cornelisz. May, in 1611 and 1612, and of which
the result was still unknown (1). The attention is
finally directed to the route, which Hudson had first
chosen with great success; many reasons are enume-
rated to show the probability of the discovery of
that

---

(1) It must however be acknowledged, that Gerritsz., in his annotations on the back of Massa's map, owned he had been rather too
sharp in his judgment; and that after the return of the travellers, —
in the edition of 1613, — he gave a detailed account of the expedition, which clearly show his appreciation of their endeavours.
Gerritsz. retracts his insolence to May in a rather remarkable way.
He wrote in the preface of his „Description of the land of the
„Samoyedes": „returning to his winterquarters the author of the
„voyage or supercargo, by divine providence, (at it appears) received
„the reward of his folly." Already on the back of Massa's map he
hastened to state: „I must note down, that I spoke rather too
decidedly in the preface, of the accident happened in Nova Francia
to the supercargo from Amersfoort, for a matter sometimes proves
to be very different from what they appear at first sight, and as
the causes, why things happen, are nearly always unknown to us,
they could not have been spoken of positively at all." But his cons-
cience and perhaps the reproval of May's friends terrified Gerritsz.
so much, that he resolved to paste in the copies of the book
still in his possession, on the unhappy words a slip of paper, and
made the sentence run thus: „They retreated to their winter-
quarters, where they searched nearly the whole coast to the
Norenberga, where one of their supercargoes and six of his companions were killed with arrows." This last version is re-produced
in this edition, so that the above mentioned words, on the back
of Massa's map, are unintelligible.

that new route; and among the advantages result-
ing from it, Gerritsz. points out, especially, the opportunity of visiting the almost unknown southern continent.

After this introduction, which bears right on to the
object Gerritsz. had in view, follow the two pieces
of Massa. It has already been stated above, that the
first work treats of the oldest commercial relations of
Russia with Siberia, and of the conquest which then
soon followed of that country. Other particulars of
this matter may be found in the interesting work of
Dr. Hamel entitled »Tradescant der Aeltere in Russ-
land, 1618." Massa's second composition, more extensive than the first, mentions the commercial roads
from Russia to Siberia and describes the manners
and customs of the tribes living there. According to
the title it is »translated from the Russian language
anno 1609." From the contents it appears that this
»translation" is very free. Massa speaks in it of things
which have happened to himself, and among others
of Le Maire's request to be a sharer himself in the
north-polar expedition of 1609. It is therefore most
probable that, in the composition of the work, he
had before him the above mentioned notes of the
brother of his Russian landlord, who had himself
been present at the subjugating expedition. Of a
printed original Russian copy there can be no ques-
tion here, considering the well-known secrecy of the
Russian government of those days, alluded to by
Massa

Massa himself, in every thing relating to Russian, and especially to Siberian geography.

After Massa's writings follows in the work of Hessel Gerritsz. a petition of Pedro Fernandez De Quiros, presented to Philip III. It is necessary to say a few words about this little work. Who were the first discoverers of Australia, when and how that discovery took place, is likely to remain a secret. The uncertainty prevailing on this point is still increased by the fact, that the first reporters generally do not distinguish at all, between Australia and the little known southern polar continent. It is certain however, that at a very early period we notice on the map many indications, proving that Australia, long before we were aware of this, was known in Spain and Portugal and even in France and England. While, however, silence prevails in books concerning this matter, it remains still undecided, whether the mention of Australia in these maps must be attributed to an actual discovery, or to a certain conviction of the real existence of an extensive country at the southern pole, similar to the supposition prevailing in the mind of Columbus concerning the existence of America. That conviction was so firm, that it may be considered as the cause, which induced the Spaniards and Portuguese to undertake so many voyages to those parts — enterprises which soon led to the discovery of small portions of that quarter of the globe, which is now known by the name of

3   Australia.

Australia. One of the undertakers of those travels was Alvaro de Mendana, who, on his second voyage in 1595, endeavoured to found a colony on the Solomon's island, and discovered the Marquis- and Charlotte-islands. On this voyage his mate was Pedro Fernandez De Quiros, »the last of the distinguished mariners of Spain, and whose name claims especial notice in every work treating of the early indications of Australia". De Quiros, probably a native of Evora in Portugal, is decidedly one of the most remarkable figures in the history of the oldest voyages of discovery to Australia. Just as Columbus, so he was on scientific grounds intimately convinced of the existence of a large country in the southern hemisphere; just as Columbus, he employed a great part of his life in endeavours to prevail upon the king of Spain to order its discovery to be tried. He did not desist from his efforts to persuade the Viceroy of Peru, and afterwards trying at the Spanish court at Madrid to have his plan put into effect, till at last, on the 21st December 1605, he entered the Spanish naval service and put to sea with three Spanish vessels off Callao. His voyage only led to the discovery of the new Hebrides, named by him Australia del Espiritu Santo; and he thence returned, for unknown reasons, back to Mexico. But his sub-commander Luiz Vaez de Torres continued his route and reached the Strait named after him the Torres Strait. De Quiros, after his return, immediately began to send to Philip III

new

new requests to induce him to sanction further trials
for the discovery of those countries, that were represent -
ed to be very rich. The expectations formed of his
voyage had however been very great, and the result
had proved so fallacious, that De Quiros did not succeed in obtaining his aim. He died at Panama in
1614. But his plan did not die with him. The sub-
joined printed eighth request, sent to Philip III, which
communicates many particulars on the island discovered
by him, »del Espiritu Santo", already appeared in
print in 1610 at Sevilla. Hessel Gerritsz. then reprinted
it; two French translations and an English one were
published in 1617, and the name of De Quiros is
now so well established, that Dalrymple declares that:
»the discovery of the southern continent, whenever
and by whomsoever it may have been completely
effected, is in justice due to his immortal name."

Of the three maps, inserted in Gerritsz. little book,
there is not much to be said. The reader will find
extensive reports concerning the great importance of
the last two in: Hamel, Tradescant der Aeltere —
in: Van der Linde, Isaac Massa, — and in: Asher,
Hudson the Navigator. We only just beg to remind the
reader, that the Hessel-Gerritsz.-notes on the back
of Massa's map contain by no means unimportant
matter concerning the ideas which the geographers of
that time, and particularly Plancius and Barendsz.,
entertained concerning the situation of the Ice-sea, —
and that those on Hudson's map supply us with
almost

almost the only source, whence Mr. Murphy reconstructed Hudson's plan of his third voyage in a most ingenious manner, — a reconstruction which places the fame of the renowned traveller on a firmer basis than ever before.

So much for the works, which the following book contains. The chief point of interest, of course, consists in the accounts they give us of the condition of many as yet little known lands; of the history of the tribes dwelling there and of the plans and degree of knowledge of the geographers of the seventeenth century. But besides this it is perhaps not unimportant to remark, that the accounts which Hessel Gerritsz. gives us in a passing and cursory manner contain nearly every thing, that is known to us concerning the voyages of the Netherlanders to the north between 1609 and 1614. Those statements are, it is true, exceedingly short and incomplete; but still they afford, occasionally, a greater quantity of matter than a slight and superficial perusal would at first lead one to think.

Again and again it appears more evident, at the publication of a new work about northern expeditions, that previous authors have not derived that benefit from the very important communications of Hessel Gerritsz. they might have done; and that the »Description of the land of the Samoyedes," is an inexhaustible source, whence every one that is desirous of

of knowing something about the north-polar voyages
of those times must draw, and to which he seldom
applies without bringing something new along with
him. The little work, alluded to, imparts particulars
unknown' elsewhere:

1. Concerning the voyages of Olivier Brunel to
   Novaya Zemlya. (Preface p. 2, comp. Description of Siberia p. 2.)
2. Concerning the voyage of Henry Hudson to
   Novaya Zemlya and the Hudson-river in 1609.
   (Preface p. 4—6. — Annotations on the back
   of Hudson's map. — Descriptio detectionis freti.
   p. 1—3.)
3. Concerning the voyage of Melchior Van Kerckhoven to Novaya Zemlya in 1609. (Preface p. 4. —
   Massa's Short account p. 8; comp. p. 13.)
4. Concerning the voyage of Jan Cornelisz. May
   to Novaya Zemlya and New-Netherland. (Preface p. 4. — Annotations on the back of Massa's
   map. — Descriptio detectionis freti. E. p. 1—3.)
5. Concerning the voyage of Pieter Fransz. to Hud-
   sons-bay and New-Netherland. (Descriptio detectionis freti p. 3.)
6. Concerning the first two voyages to Spitsbergen
   on the whalefishery in 1612 and 1613. (Descriptio detectionis freti. F. p. 4—6.)

I have mentioned repeatedly the »Descriptio detectionis freti." Allow me to add a word or two on
this

this subject. The work is nothing else than a translation of the »Description of the land of the Samoyeds,"
but one, remodelled and amplified. It was soon evident to the editor, that he had easily succeeded in
his work. The unhappy issue of May's enterprise,
who returned in the fall of the year 1612 from his
expedition, without having obtained, — in the two
successive summers spent in the high north, whither
he had bent his course, — any important result, by
no means invited to a repetition of the trial. And
nobody in Netherland thought of again following
Linschoten's plan, on which Kerckhoven's expedition
had again attracted public notice. The way through
the Strait of Nassau was evidently adapted to those,
who as yet knew nothing about the nature of the
route they were following; but so much more of
the extreme north had become known to the travellers of 1594—1597, that it could be no longer
required of the intrepid Dutch seamen to perform
the voyage in the circuitous and childish manner
which Linschoten had recommended in 1601. It
no longer became them, servilely to follow the line
of the Russian coast, now it appeared that way always led into thicker masses of floating ice. The plan
had become obsolete and only once· more a Dutch-
man, under the impression of the renewed publication
in 1624 of Linschoten's description of his voyage,
tried that old way again. (Cornelis Teunisz. Bosman
in 1625.) But though it was unnecessary to intimidate
the

the Netherlanders from trying either way in the
north-east, Hessel Gerritsz' little book was received
with general applause. The reports concerning Hudson's voyage to the north-west and the new fairy-
country, discovered by De Quiros, attracted the attention to such a degree, that in 1612 two reprints of
the »Description of the Samoyeds" were necessary.

As a skilful editor Hessel Gerritsz. knew directly
how to adjust his tackle to the wind. Without omit-
ting any of Massa's most important pieces, he simply
altered the title of his work, and the order of suc-
cession of the several pieces inserted in it, and thus
again directed the attention to those several parts of
his collection, which had suited the taste of the
public most. Already in a second issue of the Dutch
book, he amplified his notes of Hudson's voyage and
placed them, as a separate relation, at the commencement of the work, which, this time, retained the
same title. In the following edition, which appeared
in the same year, — now in Latin, so that the work
might be also intelligible in foreign countries — that
title was altogether changed. Hudson's voyage now
made a prominent figure. The work was called:
»Descriptio ac delineatio Geographica Detectionis Freti.
Sive, Tranfitvs ad Occafum, fupra terras Americanas,
in Chinam atq; Japonem dučturi, Recens investigati
ab M. Henr. Hudsono Anglo. Item, Narratio Ser^mo.
Regi Hispaniae fačta, fuper tractu, in quinta Orbis terrarum parte, cui Avftraliae Incognitae nomen
est,

est, recens detecto, per Capitaneum Petrum Ferdinandez De Quir. Vnà cum defcriptione Terrae Samoiedarvm & Tingoefiorvm, in Tartaria ad Ortum Freti Waygats fitae nuperq; Imperio Mofcovitarum fubactae. Amfterodami, Ex officina Heffelij Gerardi. Anno 1612. 4°." Those too, who were desirous of becoming acquainted with the adventures and wonders which the south produced, were served by Gerritsz. to their taste; the wish to discover a northern passage became the stronger on reading a title, which particularly directed the attention to the discovery of De Quiros. A part of the Latin work of 1612 thus appeared under the title of: »Exemplar Libelli fupplicis, Potentiffimo Hifpaniarum Regi exhibiti, à Capitaneo Petro Fernandez De Quir: Super Detectione quintae orbis terrarum partis, cui Auftraliae Incognitae nomen est. Item Relatio super Freto per M. Hudfonum Anglum quaesito, ac in parte detecto supra Provincias Terrae Novae, novaeque Hifpaniae, Chinam & Cathiam verfus ducturo: Vna Cum Freti ipsius quatenus iam detectum est, Tabula Navtica. Nec non Ifaaci Maffae Harlemenfis Samoiediae atque Tingoeffae regionum ad Orientem ultra Fretum Weygats in Tartaria fitarum, nuperque Imperio Moscovitico adquifitarum defcriptio. Et Tractus eiufdem Tabula Ruffica. Latinè versa ab R. Vitellio. Amfterodami Ex officina Heffelij Gerardi. Anno 1612. 4°." And when the interest thus felt, became so great, that within a year, another edition was wanted, the additions

tions the editor had occasionally made in the text, were again entirely revised and remodelled. The most important events, which had taken place in Netherland in the course of the year, with respect to northern navigation, were inserted; and the whole published towards the close of the year, under the scarcely altered title of: »Defcriptio ac delineatio Geographica Detectionis Freti, sive, Transitus ad Occafum suprà terras Americanas, in Chinam atq; Iaponem ʿducturi. Recens investigati ab M. Henrico Hudsono Anglo. Item, Exegesis Regi Hispaniae facta, fuper tractu recens detecto, in quintâ Orbis parte, cui nomen, Australis incognita. Cum descriptione Terrarum Samoiedarum, et Tingoesiorum, in Tartariâ ad Ortum Freti Waygats fitarum nuperq; sceptro Moscovitarum adfcitarum." The supplementary accounts in this last edition treat of the expedition of May, who had returned in the latter part of 1612, and describe in a few words the plan of the voyage to the north in 1613 (Pieter Fransz. c. s.), and further, many particulars are added about the island of Spitsbergen, now rendered prominent, since 1612, by the whale-fishery, which had commenced in that year. The attack of the English on the Netherland whalers, in the summer of 1613, was at the same time censured in the most violent terms, and the English Company threatened with reprisals. This however, drew down upon Hessel Gerritsz. a reprimand from the Netherland owners of the vessels.

They

4

They felt themselves much too weak, openly to resist the far more numerous English whalers; and considered themselves as implicated in this attack of the cartographer on James I, who felt already highly displeased with the competition his subjects had to endure on the part of the Netherlanders in the Ice-sea. — To avoid, if possible, the dreaded consequences of his imprudence, Hessel Gerritsz. added to the still extant copies of his last edition, a few pages, in which he owned, in very humble terms, to have erred in his judgment, and highly extolled the forbearance of the Netherland merchants, who expected the maintenance of their rights only from the gracious clemency of the king of England. To substantiate this good right, Hessel Gerritsz. at the same time handed over a short abstract, which his friend Plancius had drawn up, and in which, on geographical grounds, the honour of Heemskerck and Barendsz. as the discoverers of Spitsbergen, was fully vindicated.

In this way the little pamphlet of Hessel Gerritsz. became considerably enlarged.

It was however, in its original form, that it was generally known, and everywhere spread. Already in 1613, we meet with two German translations, in the collection of diaries of voyages of De Bry and in Megiser's Septentrio Novantiquus. In 1614, a third translation followed in the collection of Hulsius. (Part 12) An English version appeared in 1624, in the well-known work

of

of Purchas. The collection was furthermore reprinted no less than five times in Dutch works, (1) and
the spread of the work went even farther than this.
One can scarcely take up any volume, written in the
seventeenth century about the northern passage,
without finding the visible traces that the pamphlet,
written by Hessel Gerritsz. was the head-fountain
and often supplied the only spring of information.
It not unfrequently happened that the text was, either
partially or entirely, simply re-printed, without the
writer's name being mentioned. The contents of the
interesting work may thus be at last considered as
the common property of the learned. The book itself
however, long remained little known, and only very
recently it attracted again the general attention.
Meanwhile copies of it had become very rare, and it
cannot but be very welcome to the lovers of geography
and history, to know that it is now at last reprinted
in its original form, devoid of all additions, altera-
tions or curtailments, which such a work as this is
so likely to undergo, at the appearance of every new
edition in large collections; and especially in translations, such as the seventeenth century could fur-
nish forth.

UTRECHT,   S. MULLER Fz.
1 *September* 1874.

_____

(1) In the work entitled: Commencement and Progress of the
East-India Company, — in the collection of Hartgers, — in the
edition of Jan Jansz., — in Saeghman's „Description of Muscovy", —
and in Witsen's „North- and East-Tartary."

Beschryvinghe

Vander

Samoyeden Landt
in Tartarien.

Nieulijcks onder 't ghebiedt der Moscoviten ghebracht.

Wt de Russche tale overgheset, Anno 1609.

Met een verhael

Vande opsoeckingh ende ontdeckin-
ge vande nieuwe deurgang ofte straet int Noordwesten na de Rijcken van China ende Cathay.

Ende

Een Memoriael gepresenteert aenden
Coningh van Spaengien / belanghende de ontdeckinghe ende gheleghenthept van 't Land ghenaemt Australia Incognita.

t' Amsterdam / bp Hessel Gerritsz. Boeckvercooper / opt
Water / inde Pascaert / Anno 1612,

Prov. Salomonis 16 Cap.

Des menschen herte slaet zynen wegh aen :
Doch de Heere alleene gheeft dat hy voozt gaet.

Tot den Leſer.

DE apparentien ofte ſchijnſelen van
baet ende voozdeel hebben de men-
ſchen altoos beweecht om onbekende Landen ende Volcken te gaen
beſoecken. Alſoo hebben de ſchoone
Pelterpen (die ons van de Ruſſche
Cooplieden ghebzacht wozden) on-
ſe Cooplieden begeerich ghemaeckt om haer Landen/
die ons onbekent waren/te ronnen doozrepſen/daer toe
ſy eenighſins gheholpen zijn dooz een repſe die van de
Ruſſen beſchzeven is van der Moſcouw op Colmogro/
ende van daer op Petzoza/daer de Volcken Anno 1518/
t'Chziſten Gheloove ontfanghen hebben/ende voozder
tot de Obp/ende noch al wat verder over/ daer al eenighe fabulen in ghemenght zijn geweeſt van Slataba-
ba/t'gulden Oud-wijf met haer kinderē/ende de mon-
ſtreuſe menſchen over de Obp. Deſe Ruſſche beſchzy-
vinghe is van Sigiſmund van Herberſteyn/ Ozateur
van Keyſer Maximiliaen/in zijn Boecken vande Moſcoviſche Landen/vertaelt ende uptghegheven. Daer-
nae heeft Antonis Wied een Caerte van Ruſſenlandt
gemaeckt/dooz de inſtructie van eenen Joannes Latz-
ky/eertijds een van de Moſcoviſche Pzincen/die om de
op-roeren nae't over-lyden van Joannes Baſilius/ de
Gzoot-vozſt in Moſcovien/in Polen ghevlucht was/
welcke Caerte aen eenen J. Coper/ Raedts-heere van
Dantzick / vereert / ende met Ruſch ende Latijnſch
ſchzift uptghegeven is/in der Wilda; Anno 1555. Hier
nae iſſer noch een Caerte van dit Ruſſenland gemaeckt
dooz d'Enghelſchen / die in deſe quartieren ghetraffi-
queert hadden. Deſe Caerten ende Beſchzyvinghen
dan/ſoodanich als die zijn/ende de naeder kenniſſe die

A 3   men

men becomen hadde/hebben Olivier Bunel van Bruſ-
ſel geboortich / met een ſcheepken van Euchupſen upt-
ghelockt om derwaerts te ſeylen / die daer om ende by
gheſworven / ende in de Petzora veel Rijckdom van
Pelteryen / Ruſglas ende Chriſtal de Montagne ver-
gadert had/die met de ſchuyt in de Riviere Petzora ver-
droncken zijn. Hier nae/ alſoo de voorgaende tochten
der Enghelſchen/ende van Olivier Bunel/ die oock in
Coſtinſarck op nova Sembla gheweeſt had/onſe Hollanders beluſt maeckt en/ghelockt zijnde door de rijckdommen van China ende Cathay / daer toe ſy langhs
deſe cuſten hoopten een wech te vinden / ſoo hebben de
E. M. Heeren Staten der Vereenichde Provincien
twee ſchepen derwaert gheſonden/die met Jan Huyge
van Lintſchoten nae Weygats ſouden gaen/ende twee
die met Willem Barentſz. door de beweginge van M.
Petrus Plancius nae't Noorden boven nova Sembla
om ſouden zeylen. Maer Willem Barentſz. is op
de hoochte van 77 graeden by d'Eylanden van Oran-
gen/tuſſchen t'Land ende t'Ys beſet zijnde / op den eerſten dach van Auguſtus wederom ghekeert ; ende Jan
Huyghen is al heel de Strate van Weygats door-ghe-
zeylt / ende noch vijftich mylē verder/die om dē Noord-
ooſten Wind/ende om't verloop van't Jaer oock weer-
ghekeert zijn. Welcke beyde t'naeſt-volghende Jaer
1595 weder zijn uptgheſeylt / in meyninghe haer mer-
ken verder te ſtellen/ of den door-gangh heel te vinden:
maer de koude ende t'Ys haer teghen zijnde/hebben ſy
haer voornemen niet connen volbrengen/want ſy hebben t'Weygats niet connen paſſeren. Ende Willem
Barentſz. die al wat verder quam op zijn derde tocht/
Anno 1596/dan hy op d'eerſte tocht ronde gerakē/heeſ-
ter zijn ſchip op de Ys-bergē laten ſtaen tot een merck
ende eeuwighe memorie van d'uptterſte zeplage in het
Noor-

Noorden/diens abontuerſche Hiſtorie/droeve uptvaert
ende t'Volcks wonderlijcke t'huys-comſte men in hare
ghedruckte dach-ſchriften leſen mach.

Om dan de kenniſſen van de ghelegentheyd van deſe Landen (die onſe Cooplieden door deſe voorverhaelde reyſen becomen hebben) eenichſins behulpich te weſen/ſoo gheven wy haer hier in handen een verhael van de nieuwe heerſchappye der Ruſſen in de Landen van Tartaria/daer men ſal moghen ſien d'over-een-cominge met de ſeer curieuſe af-teeckeningen van Jan Huyghen / ende de verder gheleghentheyd van de Landen die gheleghen zijn over de Rivier Oby.

Neven deſe beſchryvinghe van Sibier ende t'Noorderſte Tartarien/gheven wy u oock een Caerte upt het Ruſſche ghetranſlateert van alle de by gheleghen contrepen / daer ſy ons voorghemaelt hebben de gheheele Zee by Ooſten de Weygats / ende een wech die men hout nae't Zuyden van Cathay te gaen: Doch of de paſſage te noordelijck gheleghen ware/ghelijck ſulcks upt de Caerte ſchijnt/ſo ſoude men nochtans/apparentelijck gheſproken/tot in de Oby/oft eenighe van d'ander groote Rivieren/te water connen comen: want immer worden die Cuſten van de Ruſſen met hare lodinghen ofſcheepkens bevaeren / ende reyſen dan voorts innewaert met ſchupten te Water of te Lande / daer't ſchijnt dat men merckelijcke dinghen ſoude connen te ontdecken. Doch alſo de Weygats des Somers weynich tijt opē of ontdopt is / alſt blijct by de twee tochtē die J. Huygen en̄ W. Barentſz. derwaert gedaē hebbē/ ſo en ſoude deſe opſoeckinge niet licht om doē zijn/wāt t'ſchijnt dat de natuer ons de koude ende t'ijs daer tot vpanden geſtelt heeft om onſe begeerte te bedwinghen: maer onaengeſien al d'exempelē bā ſo treſlicke perſonē/ als W. Barentſz. J. Heemſkerck en̄ J. Huyghen/ en̄ de

A 3   ſlechte

flechte reyſe die Kerckhoven gedae heeft voo2 Iſac La-
nier: ſo hebbē eenige ſom onervarē vermetele menſchē
haer verſtout/de E.H.Radē ter Admiralitept/eñ de M.
H. Statente verſoeckē/om beſtellinge op nieus te beco-
men/nae't noo2dooſtē boven nova Sembla om te ſeplē/
ſtoutlick affirmerende vā de hoochte vā 72 gr. noo2dlic/
om de lange dagen/lāgs hoe warmer te zijn: gelijc oock
gedaen heeft eenen Heliſeus Roſlin/Docto2 vā Hanou/
achter in zijn boeckken (aen de M. H. Staten geſch2e-
ven eñ gedediceert 1610 dē 22 Decēmb.)daer hp (na veel
ſottermē die hp fondeert op de Caerten die vā heel oude
tydē gemaect zijn vā Tartaria / doē de Ruſſen daer ſel-
ver noch geē kenniſſe af en haddē) ſept:dattet je nāher dem
Polo je wermer zu Sommerzeitten is / vnd datter kein verhin-
dernuß den Schiffen des Eyſes oder kālte halben furfallen kan.
Ende onſe lieden meenden noch wel dat de Son eerder daer
bp Noo2den nova Sembla zout ſoude maken dan ijs / ſoo ſp
ſepden. Met deſe opinien zijn ſp 1611 int voo2jaer uptgeſeplt
om verre bobē nova Sembla om te gaen/eñ van daer/ſo haer
Caerten hielden/3.3.ooſt aen/nade ſtrate van Anian/eñ voo2t
nae't lang geſochte Cathap eñ China: maer ten iſſer niet toe
gecomē dat ſp ſien mochtē hoe goet ofte ondeugende dat haer
Caerten gemaeckt waren: wāt alſo ſp te b2oech inde tijt upt-
gevarē/eñ tegē haer meninge van't ijs bedwongen weſende/
in Coſtinſarck aen nova Sembla gecomē zijn/eñ ſo zijnſe bāt
ijs beſchadicht in Moſcobia gelopen om haer te repareren:
Van daer zijn ſp/ſonder verder te attenterē/ nae de cuſtē van
Canada/tuſſchen Virginia eñ Terra nova/geſeplt /om winter lage te leggen ; daer ſp meeſt al de cuſten beſo2cht hebben tot aē
de No2enbega/daer een van haer Comiſſen met 6.andere met pplen
doo2ſchoten is. Van dit geſelſchap is t'eene ſcheepkē thups
gecomē/eñ t'ander is weder nae't Noo2dē/om beter haer nie-
ning te boldoen. Maer alſo de Engelſchen/na deſe voo2-
ſepde toehten van W.Barentſz. noch etlijcke p2oefſtuckē in't
Noo2dooſten gedaen haddē/ ſo hebben de H.Bewinthebberen
van d'Ooſt Indiſche compagnie nu eenige jarē geleden/der-
waert geſondē eenē genaēt M2. Hudſon/die mits dat hp in't
Ooſten geē wech en vont/nae't Weſten geſeplt is/vā daer hp
                                                                 ſonder

sonder profijt in Engheland is aengecomen: daer nae als hem d'Engelsche weder hebben uytgesonden/heeft hy merckelijck meerder voorspoed ende minder geluck ghehadt: want als hy naer veel moeytens ontrent 300 Duytsche mijlē by Westen Terra de Baccalaos was gecomen/ende daer Winter lage gelegen hebbende op de hoochte van 52 grad. willende verder poogen/is hy/ met al zijn Overheyt op't Schip/van't Scheeps-volck aen Land geset/die sonder verder te willen/ t'huys gecomen zijn/diens af-tekeninghen wy u hier achter byghevoecht hebben/hopende dat wy van de schepen die nu derwaert gesonden zijn / noch verder bescheyt ende tydinge van een heele doorgang sullen becomen/ waer door sy souden vercrygen een eeuwighe eer ende fama/ om dat soo lange jaren soo veel machtige Lieden ende verstandighe Piloten ghetracht hebben / om door een nieuwe corte wech te comen tot de rijckdommen van Cathay/China/de Molucké/ ende Peruaensche Volcken. Onder welcke gheweest zijn Martin Forbisher ende Joannes Davis/ die Anno 1585/ 86/ 87/ tusschen Terra nova ende Groenland Noordwaert opgheseylt zijn tot op de 72 graden/dan door't Ys weergehouden/ zijn sy/sonder yets gedaen te hebben dat tot haer voornemen dienstich was/t'huys ghekeert.

De hope van dese nieu-gevonden doorgang of strate boven Terra nova van Mr. Hudson opgedaen/is ghesterckt door de getuygenissen der Virginianen eñ Floridianen/die vastelick affirmerē ten Noordwesten van haer Lant een groote Zee te zijn/daer sy schepen seggē gesien te hebben/gelijck de schepen van d'Engelschen. Men leest oock by Josephus d'Acosta int 12 capit. des derden Boecx vant naturael van West-Indien/dat de Spaengiaerts meenen dat d'Engelse Capiteyn Thomas Candisch van dese doorgang goede kennisse ghehadt

hadt heeft: Oock seyt men dat de Spaengiaerden desen wech soecken onbekent te houden/en̄ dat eenige vā
den haren/comende van de conqueste der Philippinen/
doo₂ desen wech zijn t'huys ghecomen / daerom dat de
Coning Philippus II een sterck fo₂t heeft laté timme-
ren boven aen Mar Vermejo by Westen nieu G₂ana-
da/om te verhinderē dat onse natie ofte eenige van zijn
vpandē doo₂ desen wech hem zijn rijckdommen/die hy
aen Mar del Zur met v₂ede besit/niet en souden comen
afhandich te makē/somē ons voo₂ de waerheyt vertelt.

Dese wech dan/ist datse vervolgt ghelijck die sich op
doet/ sal d'onse een toepat wesen niet alleen na de Chi-
nen/Molucken oft Peru/maer oock om te gaen besien
wat voo₂ Volcken aen de Zuyd-zyde vande Zuyd-zee
woonen/wat Havenen en̄ wat Waren dat daer te vinden zijn/daer sy aller wegen goede ververschinge vinden sullē/t'sy dat sy gaen aen d'Eylanden daer dē Bis-
schop van Quito hē geweest heeft/ daer af ons gerap-
po₂teert is vā eē onser lantsliedē die daer geweest heeft
met dien Bisschop/de welke oock veel van sulcx vertelt
heeft aen den Advocaet Barneveld/ende den E.H. Be-
winthebberen van de Oost-Indische Compagnie/ofte
oock ist dat sy gaen aen't vaste Lant/daer ick u hier een
discours ende vertellinge af levere/hopēde dat sulcx sal
aēgenaem wesen by alle die geerne haer traffique souden doen in't achterste der aerden/ende oock by alle die
lust hebben om den Aerd-cloot ende zijn Inwoonders
hoe langhs hoe meerder te kennen/welcke kennisse ick
wensche by uwe E. te wassen tot hare volcomentheyd/
en̄ dat die u b₂enge rijckdom en̄ onverganckelicke eere.

Uwe aldervlytichste Dienaer

Hessel Gerritsz. van Assum,

Liefhebber der Geog₂aphie,

Copie

Vande beschrijvinge der

Landen Siberia, Samoieda ende Tingoesa,

met oock de weghen upt Moscovia derwaert Oost
ende Oost ten Noorden aen/ soo het daghelijcks
bereyst wordt vande Moscoviten.

Aer woont een Volck in Moscovia/
die ghenaemt worden de kinderen van
Aniconij/ende zijn van Boerser afcomst/
gesproten van een Land-man Anica ge-
naet / desen Anica rijck zijnde vã Land/
woonde ontrent een Riviere/ Witsogda
geheeten/ de welcke inde Riviere Duyna vloeyt / die 100 mylen van daer inde
witte Zee valt/ by Michael Archangel / een Slot alsoo ghenaemt.

Desen voorsz. Anica dan/rijck zijnde/ als verhaelt is/had-
de oock veel kinderen/ende was vã God van alles wel ver-
sien/ende ten vollen gesegent/dan met groote begeerlijckheyt
geprickelt/willende geerne weten/ wat voor Landen besaten
ende bewoonden de Volckeren die jaerlijcks in Moscovia
quamen handelen met costelijcke Pelterijen ende veel andere
Waren/oock vremt van spraeck/van kleedinge/Gods dienst/
ende manieren/ noemende haer Samoieden / ende oock veel-
derley andere namen haer gevende : Dese quamen soo de Riviere Witsogda jaerlijex af-drijven met haer Coopmanschap-
pen/manghelende met de Russen ende Moscoviters inde steden Osoyl ende Vstinga op de Duyna/dat als-doen ter tijdt
den Stapel was van als/oock van Pelterijen. Desen Anica
dan (als voorzen verhaelt) was begeerlijck om te weten van
waer sy quamen/ende waer haer wooninghe was/ ende wel
denckende datter groote rijckdommen te halen waeren/ aen-
ghesien de schoone Pelterijen/ diese jaerlijcks brochten/groo-
te schat bedroeghen/heeft stils wyghens alliantie ende vrunt-

B

schap

schap ghemaeckt met sommighe deser Volckeren / ende oock
eenighe van zyne Slaben ende knechten / tot 10 ofte 12 toe/
met haer in haer Lant gesonden/bebelende de selbe/datse alle
t'Landt datse door-reysden / alles wel neerstelijck bespieden
souden/ende oock alle haer manieren/wooningen/leben ende
ghebaerden wel ordentelijck souden op-teeckenen/ om so van
alles goedt rapport te doen / als sy weder t'huys souden co-
men/d'welck eens gheschiet zynde / heeft hyse/ dieder geweest
waren/wel ghetracteert/ ende oock goede gunste toe-ghedra-
ghen / dan heeft haer neerstelijck bevolen te swyghen / ende
oock heeft hy't neerstelijck by hem gehouden/ sonder yemant
daer van te vermanen / maer heeft het Jaer daer aen volghende meerder partye daer heenen ghesonden/ oock eenighe
zyner Vrienden/met Coopmanschap van kleynder weerden/
als Duytsche Cramerye/Bellen ende dierghelijcke dinghen:
dese zyn oock met gereyst/ende hebben't oock gelijck als d'andere alles wel door-snuffelt ende doorsien/ende reysden tot de
Riviere Oby toe/door vele Woestynen/ende verscheyden Ri-
bieren/die daer vele zyn / ende maeckten met sommighe Sa-
moyeden aldaer groote Vruntschap ende Alliantie/ ende ver-
namen oock dat de Pelterie daer van kleynder weerde was/
ende dat daer rijckdommen te halen waeren : Oock saghense
dat sy gheen Steden en bewoonden/ maer dat sy met troupen
soo by malcanderen leefden seer breedsamich/ende werden ge-
regeert van sommighe de outste onder haer ; waren oock on-
reyn in haer eten/ende leefden van't Wilt datse vongen/geen
Cozen noch Broodt kennende/ende meest al goede Schutters
met Bogen/de welcke sy van taey Hout maeckten/ ende waren voor ghesleepen steenen aen / oock sommighe met scherpe
Vis-graten/daerse t'Wilt met schooten / dat daer als nu met
menichte was: Oock naeydense met Vis-graten/ghebruyc-
kende Zenuen van kleyne Ghedierten tot haer Draden/ ende
voeghden soo de Vellen by malcanderen/daerse haer mede be-
deckten/Somers t'bont buyten / ende s'Winters t'bont binnen draghende: Oock dectense hare huysen met Elants-huy-
den ende Zee-vellen/die by haer niet gheacht en waren. In
somma/door-saghen't alles/ende quaemen met rijckdommen
van Bont weder t'huys/ende hebbende Anica doen van alles
verstaen/

verstaen/daer hy nae wenschte/soo dreef hy met zyne Vrun-
sten eenighe Coopmanschappe op die Landen/eenighe jaren
laugh/so dat dese Aniconij heel machtich wierden/ende koch-
ten alomme veel Lants/soo dat haer de Lieden alomme ver-
wonderden van dese schrickelijcke rijckdommen/niet weten-
de waer sy van daen quamen; sy boulweden oock Kercken in
sommighe hare Dorpen: Iae namaels boudense oock eenen
schoonen Tempel inde Stadt Osoil/op de Riviere Witsogda
ghelegen/daer sy in woonden/welcken Tempel vande gront
op was van claeren witten Arduyn: In somma/en wisten
niet waer blyven met hare goederen.

Nu merckten sy oock wel wijsselijck/dat haer t'geluck moghelijck eens den rugghe bieden soude/ghelijck ghemeynlijck
in sulcke saecken ghebeuet/siende haer alomme van vremde
seer benijt/om haer rijckdommen wille/hoe-wel sy nopt pe-
mant eenighe spijt aendeden/ende dachten sulcks met groote
voorsichticheyt voor te comen/om te blyven inden graet daer
sy in waren. Nu volgende de Moscovische maniere/is datse ghemeenelijck segghen; die te Hove gheen Vrunden heeft/
gheen mensch te ghelijcken is/om dat in Moscobia/die yet
begaeft is/tsy met wat dat het oock soude moghe wesen/benijt
en belogen wort aen't Hof/so sy daer genen Vrunt en hebben/
en sonder eenich recht oft reden onderdruckt wort/ja gantsch
t'onder-gheworpen/daer-om sy rijck zijnde/hadden al eenen
Vrunt gehadt/de welcke wel een vande meeste scheen te we-
sen/ende oock was den selven genaemt Boris Goddenoof/en
was Swager vanden Keyser Fedor Ivanowitz/die doen re-
geerde/en Boris wert na des Keysers doot in zijn plactse ver-
coren/als Rusch Keyser/ghelijck breeder verhaelt wordt inde
hedendaechse beschryvinghe der Moscobischer Oorloghen.

So hebbense dan gedacht desen Boris alles te openbaren/
doende hem eerst eenige geschencken/gelijck sy gewoon waren/
en baden hem hy haer eens verhooren wilde/als hebbende een
sake t'opebaren/die't Rijcke veel profyteren soude. Boris hier
nae gauw luysterende/heeft haer veel meer minnelijckheydt
bewesen/als hy te vooren wel hadde gedaen/ende doense hem
alles verhaelt hadde van dese ondersoeckinge der Samoyed-
sche ende Siberische Landen/oock watse daer gemerct en gesien

B 2

sten hadden/ende oock wat rijckdommen het Rijcke daer aen
ghenieten soude connen / ende hem voorts alles voor-leggen=
de/ behalven datse hem niet en openbaerden/ hoe heymelijck
datse daer mede om-ghegaen waeren; oock datse haer eerst
machtich rijck ghemaeckt hadden/ dit sweghense: niettemin
begost Boris te branden van begeerlijckheyd/ ende wilde dit
ondersoecken: jae beminde haer als zijn eyghen kinderen: ja
verhief haer/ ghevende haer vrye Brieven upt des Keysers
naem/ datse mochten sonder teghens-spreken haere Landen
diese besaten/ eeuwelijck ende erffelijck ghebruycken/nae ha=
ren wil ende beliefte/ sonder eenighe schattinghe daer van te
gheven/ nu noch naemaels: Hy lietse oock in zijn stede voe=
ren/als sy by Winter-daghe in Moscou waren/wesende een
groote genade by den Moscoviten/principalijck by so mach=
tighen Vorst als Boris was/een die't gantsche Land regeer=
de.
    Boris dit wel bedacht hebbende/ heeftet den Keyser alles
ontdect/die't seer lief was/ en Boris daer door noch meer eer=
de/ ende gaf hem daer in te doen t'ghene hem believen soude.
Boris hier op niet slapende/ heeft eenighe Capiteynen ende
sommighe arme Edel-lieden/ende die hy gonstich was/ daer
toe ghebruyckt/bevelende haer te trecken met de ghene die de
Aniconij haer met gheven souden/en kleeden haer oock coste=
lijck als Ambassaten/haer oock met-gevende eenich krijghs-
volck/ende oock geschencken van kleynder weerden/ om aen
den Volcken te schencken/ daerse souden comen/ ende beval
haer datse alle Passagien/Rivieren/ Bosschagien ende plaet=
sen wel op-teeckenen souden/ oock de namen vande selve/ op
datse wisten alle goet rapport daer van te doen/als sy souden
weder-comen; ende beval haer oock minlijck te handelen/met
de Volckeren bequaem om te gaen/ een bequaeme plaets te
bespien/omme naemaels/soo't moghelijck waere/daer eenige
Sterckte oft Castelen te maken/ ende datse immers eenighe
vande Lieden soude maken in Mosco te brengen/soo't eenig=
sins moghelijck ware: Ende alsoo zijn sy upt Mosco getroc=
ken/wel ghemaeckt van cleederen/gheweer ende gheld/ oock
gheschencken/en quamen tot Witsogda/ by-de Aniconij/ die
oock Volck toe-maeckten om met haer te trecken; oock veel
kinderen

kinde ren ende bꝛunden van haer trocken mede daer heenen.
Daer ghecomen zijnde/hebbense gedaen nae dat haer was
bevolen/ende hebben den Volcke aldaer groote bꝛundtſchap
beweſen/ond erſoeckende neerſtelijck wie bp haer de geſienſte
waren/ende hebben die eere aengedaen / ende ſchoncken haer
veel dingen van klepnder weerden/die bp haer ſeer rijckelijck
ende coſtelijck ſcheenen te weſen: jae verbepdē haer met groote jupchen en roepen/vallende te voete vooꝛ de gene die't haer
gaven/ſiende de ſelve ſoo coſtelijck ghecleedt zijnde/t'ſelve on-
ghewent te ſien / en mepnden dattet Goden waeren : Maer
alſo de Moſcoviten vooꝛ Tael-mannen ſpꝛaken/t'welck Za-
moieden waren/ die eenighe Jaeren hadden ghewoont bp de
Moſcoviſche Boeren op Doꝛpen/ende alſoo de ſpꝛake geleert
hadden/gaven haer te kennen van haeren Kepſer/ſegghende
de ſelve bp nae eenen aertſchen God te zijn : jae wel gheheel/
veel dinghen aenroerende/ die deſe arme menſchen bewogen/
om ſulcks wenſchende te ſien/ſp oock niet beter wenſchende/
namen't terſtont aen: jae noch daer bp ſepdenſe/datſe eenighe
Moſcoviters bp haer ſoo langhe in oſtagie wilden laten/ ende oock om de ſpꝛake te leeren / ſoo datſe veel Lieden met duſ-
danighe manieren op deſe zpde vande Riviere Obp aen haer
zpde creghen/ die haer den Moſcoviſchen Kepſer onderwier-
pen/ende lieten haer oock terſtondt vande Moſcoviten taxe-
ren/belovende ſaerlijcks den Moſcoviſchen Rijcke te geven/
pghelijck menſche/jae tot den kinderen toe/die maer den bo-
ghe en begonden te hanteren / een paer Sabel-vellen / die bp
haer van klepnder weerden waeren : maer bp den Moſcoviten vooꝛ een juweel ghehouden/en beloofden t'ſelve te gheven
in handen vanden ghenen die dat t'ontfanghen beſteldt ſoude
woꝛden/t'welck oock ten vollen geſchach: Ende vooꝛts trocken ſp over de Riviere Obp wel 200 mplen dooꝛ't Landt hee-
nen/ſiende veel ſeltſame Gedierten/ſchoone Fontepnen/ frap
Crupden ende Boſſchagien/ oock veelderlep Samopeden/ de
ſommighe op Elanden rpdende/ ſommighe op ſteden ſitten-
de/die van Reen ghetrocken werden/de ſommighe van Hon-
den/die ſoo ſnel liepen als Herten/in ſomma ſagen vele daer-
ſe haer van verwonderden/ende teeckenden oock alles oꝛden-
telijck op/om naemaels goet beſcheet te bꝛengen / en quamen
ſoo

soo wederomme / eenighe ghewillighe Samopeden met haer
nemende/ende lieten oock eenighe Moscoviten in haer Lant/
om de spꝛake te leeren/en zijn soo in Mosco ghecomen/daerse
van alles goet bescheedt bꝛachten aenden vooꝛsz.Boꝛis/ ende
Boꝛis aen den Keyser / ende saghen met groot verwonderen
de Samopeden aen/die sy met ghebꝛacht hadden/ de selve be-
velende te schieten/ t'welck soo fier van haer gheschach / dattet gheen mensche soude willen ghelooven : Want een pen-
nincxken cleender dan een halven stuyver / settense in cenen
Boom / ende ginghen daer soo wijt van / datse nauwelijcks
t'penninccxken / oft effen in't ghesicht conden hebben / ende
treften t'selve so menichmael / als sy de pijle daer na schoten/
sonder eens te missen/ t'welck velen dede verwonderen.
  Ten anderen zijden / saghen dese wilde lieden t'leven der
menschen in Mosco met groote verwonderinghe aen / oock
der Stadts manieren/ende meer dierghelijcke dingen: Maer
met verschꝛickinghe aensaghense den Keyser/zijnde soo costelijck gecleet/sittende so te Paerde/ oft varende so in een Coets
van veel peerden getrocken/costelijck verciert/ omringt met
memichte van groote Heeren / seer costelijck verciert/ en saghen oock seer nae alle t'krijghsvolck die met de roers soo al
in roode rocken om den troep liepen/ zijnde altijdts als den
Keyser uyt-reedt / omtrent vier-honderdt schutten by hem.
Oock hooꝛdense met verwonderinghe aen t'gheluyt der cloc-
ken/die met menichte in Mosco zijn/ oock saghense met verwonderinghe alle de costelijcke winckels in Mosco/ ende alle heerlijckheydt aldaer/ in somma/ sy meynden datse in der
Goden thꝛoon waren gheraeckt / ende wenschten alreede te
zijn by haer mede-bꝛoederen/ om haer dit alles te vercondi-
ghen/noemende haer salich te zijn / sulcken Hooft te moghen
obedieren/als den Keyser/ dicse meynden eenen Godt te zijn/
oock smaeckte haer de spijse wel/ die haer in Mosco was t'e-
ten ghegheven/ wel pꝛoevende datse haer beter smaeckte dan
rauw beesten in haer landt/oft dꝛooghen visch.
  In somma hebben den Keyser belooft hem vooꝛ Heere aen
te nemen/ende beloofden oock hare mede-bꝛoederen/verre en
by te beweghen : Ende vooꝛts baden sy den Keyser / dat hy
haer de genade doen wilde/ ende seynden haer Gouverneurs
die

die haer souden regieren / ende diese de voor-verhaelde schattinghen mochten in handen leveren: aengaende van haer af-
goderie / daer en werdt niet af verhaelt / maer bleef soo naer
haer ghewoonte/ dan ghelcove wel dat t'Christen Ghelcove
daer haest gheplant soude worden/ waert datter eenighe be-
quame Leeraers waren / en ghelcove metter tijdt t'selve wel
in't werck ghestelt soude werden/ waert dat sy niet besich en
waren/ met dese sware Oorloghen/daer sy met beladen zijn.

Zijnde dit alles gheschiet als boven verhaelt is / so zijn de
kinderen Aniconij seer verheven/en werdt haer alomme vele
vryhept gegeven/en oock bevel over eenige plaetsen/ontrent
hare Landen gelegen/die vele en groot zijn: Ja hebben lant/
hondert mijlen van malcanderen/hier en daer op de Rivieren
Duina/Witsogda/ende Soehna / so datse rijck ende alomme
vol zijn / ende worden noch daghelijcx by haer eere behouden.

En wert in Moscou gheraedtslaecht datmen herwaert/
langs en omtrent de Riviere Obi/inde vlacke velden/sterck-
ten en plaetsen upt der natueren daer toe soeckende/Castelen
moest maken / ende met crijchsvolck besetten/en diende oock
eenen generalen Gouverneur aldaer/om de Landen allengskens wijder ende wijder te versoecken/en tselve also te incor-
poreren/d'welck alles gheschiet is/ende eerst zijn aldaer ghebouwt geworden eenige Casteelen van groote balcken/upten
bosschen aldaer/ende die met aerde gevult/ende so met soldaten beset/oock werter dagelijcx veel volcx henen gesonden/ so
datter op sommige plaetsen/metter tijt heele gemeynten wa-
ren/vermengelt met Polen/Tarters/ Russchen/ ende andere
Natien.

Want alle ballingen/ende die moorders/ verraders en die-
ven waren/en allerley schuym van menschē/ die de doot ver-
dient haddē/wierden daer henen verbannē/de sommige daer
een tijt lanc gevangen gehoudē/ de sommige bevolen te woo-
nen/na dat hare misdaet groot was/ ende wierdē so allengskens groote steden van veel volckē/ dese Casteelen en groote
ghemeynten/ nu wel een Conincrijck besonder ghelijckende/
want naemaels veel arme lieden daer henen trocken/ om
datse aldaer veel vrydom hadden/ ende Landt om niet: En
dese Landt-douwe werdt Siberia ghenaemt / ende oock
                                                    werter

werter een Stadt gebouwt/diemen Siber noemde/ ende doe-
men in't eerste in Mosco hoozde banden naem Siberia/ gru-
welden de boosdaders in Mosco daer booz/ ghelijck int eerst
t'Amsterdam die't weerdich gheweest zijn booz het Tucht-
huys verschzickten. Want men sontse terstont na Sibirdam.
Nu ist so ghemeen dattet niet meer gheacht en wert/ maer de
Heeren en Edelen in Mosco zijnde in s'Kepsers onghenade
verballen/zijnder noch wel banghe booz/ dan die wozdender
somtijdts booz een tijt lanck gesonden/met Vzouw' ende Kin-
deren/ende wozt haer daer eenich goubernement bevolen/tot
dat den toozne des Gzoot-vozsts ghestilt is/als dan wozden-
se weder in Mosco ontboden.

Om nu te weten den wech upt Moscobia tot daer toe / sal
ick verbolghens/ nae vermogen/ verhalen/als hebbende niet
meer connen becomen/ ende dat noch met groote moeyte ende
vzuntschap/hebbende te Hove sommighe vzunden in Mosco/
doen ick daer woonde/die my groote jonste toe-dzoegen/ ende
my t'selve gaven/ alsoo ick lange aenhielt/ eer zijt my dozsten
gheven/ en haddet noch upt-ghecomen by tyde van Vzede in
Mosco/ t'soude haren hals ghekost hebben de ghene die't my
gaven/soodanich ist Moscovisch Volck: Want sy en moghen
niet lyden dat de secreten van haer Land ontdeckt wozden.

Een

Een cort verhael van de

Wegen ende Rivieren upt Moscovia

Ooſtwaerts eñ Ooſt ten Nooꝛden aen te Landewaert/
ſoo het nu alreede daghelijcks bereyſt woꝛt vanden Moſcoviten ; Oock de namen der Steden aldaer vanden Moſcoviten ghebouwt / met des ſelven Gouverneur oock beſet/
die dat Landt daer al-omme bewoont / op-ſoecken
ende in-nemen laet ; jae by nae tot in groot
Tartarien toe heeft laten beſoecken.

T Witſogda Soil/ van daer de Aniconij
woonen/reyſen ſy de Riviere opwaert/tot datſe comen by een Stedeken vande Moſcoviten
bewoont/datmen Jabiniſco noemt/ende is 17
dach-reyſens vande Sadt Soil/de Riviere op-
waert/dooꝛ Rivieren en Boſſchen reyſende/en-
de valt deſe Riviere Witſogda upt het gheberchte Joegoria
ghenaemt/de welcke ſtrecken upt Tartarien van't Zuyden/
tot by na de Zee nae 't Nooꝛden : Wt de ſelve geberchten valt
oock de Riviere Petſioꝛa / die inde Zee valt / op deſe zyde
Waygats.

Van Jabiniſco/ dꝛie Weecken reyſens/comenſe in een Riviere dieſe Ne-em noemen/of Stom op Duytſch/ om haeren
ſtillen loops wille tuſſchen den Boſſchen : Soo ontrent vyf
daghen met Schuyten ofte Vlotten gereyſt hebbende in deſe
Riviere Ne-em/ſo moetenſe t'goedt een myle over Land voe-
ren/want deſen Ne-em loopt eenen anderen cours als ſy reyſen moeten/ ſo datſe om der coꝛthept wille over Lant een myle weeghs reyſen / en comen ſoo in een Riviere dieſe Wyſſera
noemen/eñ deſe Riviere valt upt Steen-clippen/die de Moſcoviten Camena noemen / ende ligghen oock in't gheberchte
Joegoria/ ende reyſen ſoo met de Riviere nederwaerts 9 daghen langh / ende comen dan by een Stedeken datſe noemen
Soil Camſcop / en is vanden Moſcoviten ghebouwt tot een
ruſt-plaetſe vooꝛ de reyſende Lieden. / want ſy van hier moe-

C   ten

ten vozder te Lande repsen/ende de vooznoemde loopt boozts
haeren cours/ende valt ten lesten inde Kibiere Cam/ welcke
Cam loopt onder de Stadt Viatea in Moscobia / ende epn-
dicht haer inde groote Kibiere Kha/ of Volga/ die in Mare
Caspium bloept met 70 in-ganghen/ alles ghehoozt van per-
soonen die't ghesien ende ghesocht hebben.

Te Soil Camscop berust hebbende / soo zijnder vele Peerden metter tijdt al op ghebzocht/ende is oock alreede wel bewoont ende t'Landt rond-om met Dozpen ende Vee wel ver-
sien/al meest Kussen en Tartars zijnde/ soo nemense haer ba-
gagie op Peerden / ende repsen van daer meest over geberch-
te vol Dennen/Pijnboomen/ oock ander seltsaeme Boomen/
ende repsen dwers over een Kibiere in het gheberchte Sopba
ghenoemt/daer nae noch over eene diese Coosna noemen/loo-
pende bepde nae het Noozden. Dit gheberchte wozt by haer
in dzien ghedeelt/ende is een heel ander Lant als daer sy upt-
comen/schoonder Bosschen/vaster van Hout / ende oock veel
verschepden Crupden daer wassende / ende wozdt twee dach-
repsens langh ghenaemt Coosvinscop Camen; noch ander
twee dach-repsens woztet genaemt Cirginscop-Camen; daer
nae vier dach-repsens langh is Podbinscop Camen/ende comen dan tot een Stadt genaemt Vergateria: Dese dzie vooznoemde Woestynen wozdē meest besocht van wilde Tartars
ende Samopeden / die niet en doen dan alle kostelijck Wildt
vanghen voor den Moscoviter: Dat gheberchte Podbinscop
Camen is t'hoochste ende op veel plaetsen met sneeu bedeckt
ende wolcken/ende t'selve is seer moepelijck om repsen / maer
t'valt so allengskens seer leeghe.

Comende tot Vergateria vooznoēt/moetense hier wachten
tot in't Vooz-jaer/ wāt daer is een Kibiere Toera die't heele
Jaer aldaer ondiep is/ om datse daer eerst haren oozspronck
heeft / maer in't Vooz-jaer woztse gantsch diep vanden sneeu
des gheberchte aldaer/ende repsen dan alsoo met booten ende
schupten boozder.

Dese Stadt Vergateria is d'eerste Stadt in't Lant Sybe-
ria/ ende wiert eerst ghebouwt over 21 Jaren / met meer andere Steden al-daer ontrent/ende is oock wel bewoont/oock
bouwense Laudt ghelijck men in Moscobia doet.

Oock

Oock isser eenen Gouberneur al-daer / die alle voor-jaren menichte ban Proviandan ende Cooren sendt al-omme voor die Rivieren inden gantschen Syberischen Lande / in alle Casteelen ende plaetsen daer Soldaten ende krijghsvolck is: Oock ober de Oby in allen Forten ende plaetsen aen't Moscovisch Volck / want sy aldaer niet en bouwen noch ter tijdt / ende de Samopeden leven ban het Wildt als verhaelt is.

Nu dese voor-schreven Riviere Toera af-drijbende / comense naer vijf daghen in een Stadt / Japhanim ghenaemt / oock ober twee Jaeren ghebouwt / ende met Volck gheplant.

Tot Japhanim comende / reysense voorder inde selve Toera / ende twee daghen gherepst hebbende / begint haer dese Riviere seer kromme te draeyen / soo datse haer dickmaels moeten oversetten inde selve Riviere ober Landt / om de rechte te hebben / ende om der cortheyt wille.

Ende nu woonen hier altijdt Tartren ende Samopeden / die daer omtrent Vee houden / daer sy van leven: Oock houwense Booten.

Ende ten lesten ban dese Riviere Toera comense in een groote Riviere Tabab / zijnde by naer twee hondert mylen ban Vergateria / maer sy reysen tot Tinnen toe / een Stadt vol Volcks / oock bande selbighe voor-verhaelde ghebouwt / dan bele reysen ooc wel ban Japhanim met slede inde Winter tot Tinnen in twaelf daghen tijdts / ende hier gheschiedt nu grooten handel ban Pelterpen met den Moscoviten / teghen de Tartren ende Samopeden / ende dese plaetse is goedt voor de ghene die maer een half Jaer uyt en wil zijn: Maer bele soecken 't wyder / sae tot verre ober die Riviere Oby / soo nae t Oosten als nae't Zuyden.

Van Tinnen comen tot Tobolsca / het Hooft der Syberische Steden / ende al-daer is den Stoel Syberia / ende den opperst en Viceroy bande Moscoviten / ende daer moeten alle Steden haere schattinghen Jaerlijcks brenghen / soo wel ban d'ander zyde de Oby / als op dese zyde / ende wordt daer oock versamelt / ende soo met gheleyde Jaerlijcks met Casacken en Krijgs-volck nae Mosco gesonden / eñ hier wort oock

C 2   strenghe

strenghe recht ghehouden. En moeten oock alle Gouverneurs in Samopeda en Siberia desen obedieren. Oock gheschiet daer grooten handel in alle dinghen / upt Moscovia
daer ghebracht : Oock comender Tarteren upt het Zupden/
heel wijt upt Tartaria / ende veel verscheyden Volcken / die
daer allenskens meer ende meer comen/ nae dat de fame van
dit Lant wyder ende wyder streckt / en is al vast profijt voor
de Moscoviten/ die 't met vreden soo geincorporeert heeft/ dat
hy niet en hoeft te vreesen/ soo seer zijnse den Moscoviten toe-
ghedaen/ ende oock zijnder alomme Kercken/ wilde God dat
den wreeden Spaengiaert America in plaetse van zyne on-
menschelijcke tyrannie/ met sulcken vrede in-ghecreghen had-
de/ soo mocht men hem noch eenichsins t'selve gunnen / want
men veel meer van sulcks met vruntschap sal connen vercry-
ghen/ ghelijck ick t'selve ghemerckt heb / en noch daghelijcks
vanden Moscoviten hoore en aenmercke/ dan met wreede ty-
rannie oft ghewelt/ etc.

Dese voornoemde Stadt Tobolsca leydt op de groote Riviere Prtijs ghenaemt/ die seer sterck valt upten Zupden/ ende loopt wel soo snel als de Donouw doet/ ende valt inde Riviere Oby/ ende sy schijnt met Oby upt een geweste te romen;
aë d'ander zyde de Stadt loopt de Riviere Tobol voornoemt/
daer de Stadt de naem af heeft.

Inde Riviere Tobol comt een vallende Riviere / die recht
upt het Noorden upt het gheberchte by den Zee-cant schijnt
te vallen/ ende wort vanden wilden geheeten Taffa/ en op de
selve Riviere hebben de Moscoviten nu onlancx een Stadt
gebouwt/ Pohem genaemt/ ende hebben deselve beset met allerley volck upt de Sibierische Steden / en dat om oorsaecke
datter soo schoone Landouwe omtrent is/ oock schoone Bosschagien zijnde vol Wilt / van Luppaerden/ Lossen/ Vossen/
Swerte/ oock Sabels en Maters: En dese Stadt leyt twee
weken repsens van Tobolsca / noortwaert de Riviere Prtis/
daer van verhaelt is/ loopt oock inde Oby/ t'wee weken repsens van Tobolsca: Ende op de Mont was eertijts oock een
Stadt ghebouwt/ die ghenaemt was Olscop-gorot/ maer is
naemaels door 't bevel des Gouverneurs in Sibirien ghe-
rupmt/ niet segghende waerom : Ick dencke t'is geweest om
de

de koude/oft om datse na haer meyninge/ te na den Zee-cant
stondt / breesende datter eenich overval ofte veranderinghe
mocht gheschieden: Ende also upt de groote Riviere Obp een
groot water loopt/ombangende een groot deel Lants/ gelije
eenen arm/en balt t'selve so weder inde Obp/ maeckt soo een
groot Eplandt / en hebben op dit Eplandt weder een ander
Stadt ghebouwt/ in plaetse bande gherupueerde / ende hebbense Zergolt gheheeten/zijnde ontrent 50 mplen opwaerder
als d'ander ghestaen hadde.

En als sp van daer door de Riviere opwaerts repsen/ghe-
bzupckense wepnich zepl op hare Booten/t'sp om datter wepnich Wint is/ of om't hooghe Lants wille / hoe-wel de Obp
alsints groot ende bzeedt is/maer trecken de Booten op/ghe-
lijckse meest in alle plaetsen door de Rivieren in Moscovien
repsen/ en repsen ban Zergolt ontrent 200 mplen opwaerts/
en comen dan tot een Casteel/ghenoemt Norinscop/ dat over
13 Jaeren ghebouwt wierdt/ als den grooten Gouverneur
Volck upt Sibirien sant/ om Landen op te soercken/bequaem
zijnde booz menschen/ ende om steden te bouwen /en hebben
doen alsoo daer een Casteel ghebouwt / daer eenich Krijghsvolck op is/ een plapsante/ ghesonde ende warme plaetse/ en
seer bzuchtbaer / daer oock veel frap Ghedierte ende Ghevo-
ghelte is: Het lept in't Zupd-oosten/ ende is naemaels oock
een Ghemepnte ghewozden/en haer wiert bevolen noch wpder en wpder/nae de warmte opwaert/ t'Landt te bespieden;
maer haer is altijdt bevolen met Bzuntschap te handelen/en-
de den Volcke bzundelijck te tracteren/ diese souden ontmoe-
ten/ oft vinden / om soo wpder ende wpder Volck te hebben.
Alsse nu met troepen te Lande-waert in repsden / tot over de
400 mplen/saghense alomme schoone Landouwe/ maer geen
menschen/maer al woest Landt.

Van alsoose bp de 200 mplen quamen door de Riviere Obp
op-repsende/hebben (nu geleden 10 jaren) eene schoone plap-
sante Landouwe ghebonden /oock seer warm / sonder datter
eenighe onbequaemhept was/ende oock wepnich Winter/ of
bp nae gheen/en sp daerom weder in Siberia ghecomen zijn-
de/hebben beroozsaeckt gheweest t'selve inder Mosco te ont-
bieden/ende regeerde aldaer den Bozis Goddenoof / de welc-

C 3   ke de

ke de ſaecke ſeer behertichde/ende beval oock terſtont dat den
Gouverneur upt Siberia daer volck henen ſoude ſenden/om
daer een Stadt te laten bouwen / het welck gheſchiede / ende
daer is een ſchoon Caſteel gemaeckt / met noch eenighe huy-
ſen/ſo dattet nu een ſchoone Stadt is/ ende wozt Toom ghe-
naemt/om datſe namaels ghehoozt hebben/datter mennichte
Tartaren op deſelve plaetſe ghewoont hebben / ende ſoo ſoude die Stadt van den Tartaren / ſoo den naem ontfanghen
hebben / om haer plapſancy wille / ende deſe Tartaren hadden eenen Coninck onder haer / die Altijn ghenaemt was/
ende ſoo wozdt deſe Stadt dickmaels noch beſpzonghen van
diverſche volckeren die haer derwaerts int veldt onthouden/
dan nu iſſe ſoo machtich/dattet metter tijt oock wel een clepn
Coninckrijck mocht wozden.

Nu tuſſchen dit Caſteel Nozinſcoz/ende deſe Stadt Toom
en Sibirien vindenſe noch daghelijcks te Lande-waert veel
diverſche Volckeren / die haer Oſtachij noemen / die nu
oock al metten Moſcoviten/ Tartaren / ende Samopeten in
Siberia haer vereenighen / ende met vziendtſchappe handelen / bzenghende ſommighe oock Goudt ende andere din-
ghen/ende hebben onder haer veel Coninghen/zijnde die ghelijck de Indianen / te weten / de clepne die in Ooſt-Indien
woonen / ende niet de groote: In ſomma de Moſcoviten
comen ſoo wijdt dat Quartier upt / dattet te verwonde-
renis.

Oock zijnder veel Caſteelen en Stedekens tuſſchen de
Riviere Oby ende Pztis/ dewelcke in de ſelvetijdt / oft wepnich daer nae ghebouwt wierden / als Tobolſca ghebouwt
wierdt/ende zijn nu oock gantſch rijck/ zijnde ghemengt met
Moſcoviten / Tartaren ende Samopeden/ die tamme zijn/
ende wozden deſelve Steden ghenaemt Tara / omtrent welcke plaetſe / die Rivieren Oby ende Pztis / thien dach repſen
van malcanderen zijn: oock een Stadt die Jozgoet genaemt
is/ ende die is ghetimmert over vierthien ofte vijfthien ja-
ren/ oock Beſou / ende Manganſoiſcopgozad / ende ligghen
deſe booznoemde Steden opwaert naer het Supden/ maer
op de Weſt-zijde der Riviere Oby/ ſoerken de Inwoonders
noch daghelijcr wijder en wijder te comen. Herwaert op deſe
                                                              zijde

zijde de Obp/ ligghen de Steden Tobolsca/ Sibier/ Beresai/
ende meer andere op verschepden Kibieren ligghende/ ende
wozt noch daghelijcr meer ghebouwt.

Maer de Steden Narim ende Toom / ligghen op d'ander
zijde de Kibiere Obp : Hier ghebzupcken de lieden veel Reen
in haer steden/ oock snelle honden/ die sp veele met visch spij-
sen/daer se na haer oozdeel seer sterck van wozden zijnde ghe-
dzoochden Roch : Maer Jozgoet booz-verhaelt light in de
Obp op een Eplandt.

Nu van Narim op-waert na het Oosten/ de Kibiere ghenaemt Telt / daer hebbense oock een Casteel ghebouwt ende
noemen t'selve Comgofscop/en besettent oock met volck: Van
dit Casteelken en Narim/ zijnse dooz t'bevel des Siberi-
schen Gouverneurs / over seven jaren gheleden / ghesonden
met sleden en Peerden recht nae het Oosten / om aldaer te
soecken ofter eenighe onbekende Volckeren haer onthiel-
den / ende repsden wel ontrent thien weecken lanck / recht
Oostwaert dooz groote woestijnen/ bindende alomme schoone Landouwe/ oock schoone boomen/ende veel diversche Kibieren: maer omtrent de tijdt voozsz. gherepst hebbende/heb-
bense op den belden eenighe hutten ghesien / bindende oock
veel vergaderinghe van menschen/ dan alsoo sp Samopeden
ende Tarters tot Lepdts-lieden hadden / die oock moghelijck de weghen wel dooz-loopen hadden/en warense niet be-
schzoomt.

Maer comende omtrent de menschen bewesen haer groote
eerbicdinge ende cregen de Samopeden ende Tarters so veel
van haer te verstaen/ datse haer selven met de name Tingoesp noemden / en woonden al langhs de groote Kibiere diese
Jenifcea noemden/ en wesen haer te spzupten upt het Supd-
Oost/dan wiften haer begin niet/en was de Kibiere grooter
dan de Obp/oock hadden dese lieden groote croppen onder de
kinne klockende met haer spzaecke als de Kalcoetten/t'scheen
dat de Samopeden haer spzake in veel verstonden/ ende sp de
Samopetse spzake met heel ongelijc en was/maer daer naer
seer helde.

Dese Kibiere Jenifcea / veel grooter zijnde dan de Obp/
heeft aende Oost-zpde groote gheberchten / daer onder oock
Dper-

Ober-berghen zijn / die Swebel ofte Solpher upt-werpen: Maer op dese zyde naer het Westen daer ist leeghe. schoone Landouwe / seer playsant van alderley Cruyden / Boomen/ liesselijcke Bloemen/ende diversche vzende Vzuchten : Oock heel seltsaem Gheboghelte/het welcke leeghe Land wozt wel by de 70 mylen weeghs ober-loopen inde Lenten vande Ri= biere Jeniscea/eben(nae wy verstaen)ghelyck de Nyl in E= gypten doet/ende dese Tingoesy dit wetende/onthouden haer ober d'ander zyde soo lange op de gheberghten/ tot dat de Ri= biere valt/ende comen dan weder in dese schoone leeghe Lan= den met alle haer Vee.

Dese Tingoesy was minnelijck Volck/ende onderwozpen haer oock den Goubcrneurs die de Samopeden regheerden/ ende dit al dooz de Samopeden haet daer toe beweghende/ en noemden die by nae Goden te zijn. Men conde niet merc= ken wat Gods-diensten dese Lieden hadden/ noch men heeft het noyt connen bernemen/alsoo dooz onachtsaemheydt van= de Moscobiten alle dinghen ten nausten niet bespiet en wozt.

Ten verwondert my oock gantsch niet/ dat jaerlijcx Way= gats so verstopt is met ijs in't Noozden/aenghesien de groo= te Ribieren Oby ende Jeniscea soo schzickelijck veel ijs upt= spouwen/ende noch meer ontallijcke andere Ribieren/ diens namen men niet en weet/de welcke soo ontallijcke dickte van ijs uptwerpen/dattet ongheloosslijck is/ want in't Vooz-jaer dzybet ijs omtrent den Zee-cant somtijdts heel Bosschen met hem weech/van weghen zyn dickte ende menichte/waer dooz comt datmen aende stranden van Waygats so veel Hout al= lesins siet aenghedzeben ligghen : Oock zynde in de engde by noba Sembla/ de upterste konden/soo en ist niet wonder dat= tet daer op-hoopt dooz de enghde/ende oock noch bzieft/ ende soo dicht in malcanderen sich settet / tot dat het de dickte van 60 of ten minsten 50 vademen krijght/ghelyck dit Jaer heb= ben af-ghemeten die met een cleyn schipken daer weder-om waren van Isaac le Maire uptghesonden/ die my daer oock geerne heen hadde ghehadt / maer sloech het af/want ick be= wysen wil datmender niet dooz en can/en altijts bergeefs sal wesen wat sy doen/oft moesten't anders aenlegghen.

Sy hebben oock ober dese Ribiere wyder reyse aengheno=
men/

men/maer hielent recht int Oosten/ weynich doozvenve nae't
Zupden wenden / en hadden eenighe van dese Tingoese met
haer/ van de welcke sp verstonden/ datter Zupdt-waert veel
volckeren die haer bzeemt waren / woonden / ende oock Coninghen nae dat sp verstaen conden / onder haer hadden / die
dickmaels teghen malcanderen oozloogden.

Dan niemant vernomen hebbende/ zijnse wederom ghecom-
men nae eenighe dach repsens / maer hebben de Tingoesp bevolen wijder te soecken/die't haer beloofden/en oock bziendt-
schap ende aliantie met haer maeckten/latende eenige Mos-
coviten/gheallieerde Samopeden ende Tartaren bp haer/ en
gaven haer ooc eenighe gheschencken: Dan t'volghende jaer
sonden de Tingoesp volck van haer zijde / Oost-waert op/
noch verder dan sp te bozen ghewreeft waren / en trocken met
groote mennichte daer henen / en hebben ten lesten noch een
groote Kiviere vernomen/dan niet wel so bzeet als Jeniscea
haer Kiviere/maer wel soo snel loopende/en daer eenighe daghen langs ghelaopen hebbende / ten lesten noch eenighe lieden ghesien/ die sp achterhaelden/ en sommighe ghevanghen
creghen/maer conden haer niet verstaen/dan dooz wijsen ende bedien hebbense soo veel van haer ghehoozt/ dat aen d'ander zijde dickmaels ghedonder was/seggende:Om-om/oock
datter menichte van ghetier ende gherupsch was van men-
schen/en wesen op die Kiviere/en sepden Pesida/ daer upt de
Tingoesp ende Tartars besloten dat sp de Kiviere soo noem-
den/en upt de woozden/Om-om/besloten de Moscoviten namaels / dat het ghelupdt van Clocken moeste wesen / en weder vertreckende/namense eenighe van dese lieden mede/ dan
sturven al onder weghen/t'zp van bangichepdt oft bzeese/oft
veranderinge des Lochts/daer de Tingoesp/Samopeden/en
die met haer waren/seer dzoevich om waren/want wederom
comende / sepden datter cloecke lieden waren / wel ghestelt/
clepn ooghen hebbende/ ende platte aensichten/ bzupn zijnde
upt den gheelen.

De Moscoviten in Siberia dit alles ghehoozt hebbende
vande Samopeden/ die upt Tingoesen-lant in Siberia quamen / waren seer begheerich om noch wijder te soecken / be-
gheerende volck van den Gouverneur / die haer t'selve ver-
D   gonde

gonde/ oock felfs veel Krijghs-lieden met fendende / met bevel alles wel te dooẑfiē/oock Tingoefen met te nemen/en Sa-
mopeden/oock Tarters/ende zijn fo ontrent 700 mannen heenen ghetrocken/ ober de Ribiere Oby / dooẑ der Samopeden
ende Tingoefen Land/ ober de groote Ribiere Jenefcia/ende
zijn foo booẑder ende booẑder gherepft / hebbende tot booẑ-
ganghers Tingoefen/die haer den wegh booẑ-dẑaefden / hare fpyfe veerdich onder-weghen vanghende/foo Voghels als
Reen/Gepten ende ander bẑemde Dieren / en bonghen oock
Viffchen/als t'Landt dooẑ reghen zijnde met veel fchoone Ribieren / ende zijn oock tot de booẑnoemde Ribiere Pefida ge-
comen/ ende hebben by de felve hutten op-ghefet / ende daer
eenen tijdt-lanck gheleghen / tot het Vooẑ-faer toe datfe die
Ribiere open fien wouden./ ende t'was by naer in het Vooẑ-
jaer alffe daer quamen: maer ober die Ribiere en dozften fp
niet comen / als hoozende dat haer te boozen ghefepdt was/
ende verftonden/dattet ghelupdt van Clocken was: als den
Windt van ober de Ribiere quam/hoozdenfe oock dickmaels
ghedẑeun van Volck en Peerden / ende faghen oock eenighe
feplen fomtijdts/doch wepnich/ die af-liepen / nae haer mey-
ninghe/de Ribiere onderwaert/ende fepden naemaels dat de
zeplen bier-cant waren / ghelijck ick dencke de feplen in Indien zijn; maer gheen menfchen vernomen hebbende aen die
zyde daerfe waeren/bleven daer eenighen tijdt / ende bevon-
den oock dat de Ribiere heel hooghe werdt in't Vooẑ-faer/
dan wepnich te achten / naedemael t'Landt aen bepde zyden
hooghe was: Haer herte verheuchde in't aenfien vande feer
fchoone Landouwe/zijnde in May ende Apẑil. Oock fagen-
fe veel raritept van Crupden/Bloemen/ Vẑuchten / ende felt-
fame Boomen/ Dieren ende bẑemde Voghelen: Maer alfoo
de Mofcobiters daer niet curieus en zijn/achtent felve niet/
foeckende maer pẑofijt aen allen zyden; want het zijn een deel
plompe heele menfchen.

Ende foo inde Somer zijnfe wederom ghecomen/ repfende
langhfaem: Want het was inden Herbft als fp in Siberia
quaemen / ende verkondichden alles watfe daer ghefien
ende gbehooẑt hadden/ende confirmeerden t'felve met haeren
Eede,

Alle

Alle dese voornoemde dinghen te Hove inder Mosco ver-
adverteert zijnde / hebben den Keyser Boris ende alle andere
groote Heeren haer daer over seer verwondert / met yverighe
begheerte ontsteecken zijnde / omme dit alles ten nauwsten te
doen soecken / meynde t'volghende Jaer daer Ammassadeurs
heenen ghesonden te hebben met vele gheschencken / de welke mede ghenomen souden hebben Tartren / Samopeden ende Tingoesen / om te trecken over de Riviere Pepsida / ende
te vernemen wat daer was / ende oock alliantie te maecken
met den Coninghen ende Volckeren al-daer / soo sy daer ye-
manden vonden: Haer oock bevel ghevende / alles fijn ordentelijck te verspien ende doorsien / ende op te teeckenen /
want sy conden niet verghenten van datse der Clocken ghe-
lupt ghehoort hadden: Maer dit is alles naegebleven / als
doen beginnende in Moscobia dese troubel ende Inlandtsche
Oorlogen / als inde beschrybinge des selven daer van te verstaen is.

Ick gheloove dattet het beghin van't Coninckrijck Ca-
thapa is / t'welcke paelt aen China ende Indien / dan sorghe
dat den Moscoviter daer metten hoofde tegen den muer loo-
pen sal / dan den tijt alles sal leeren / soo sy het noch naemaels
versoecken.

Dan niet te min hebben de Gouverneurs / gheduerende
de Moscobische Oorloghe / noch derwaerts eenen tocht doen
doen / daer onder veel Burghers byrwillich uyt Siberia mede trocken / ende comende inder Tingoesen Landt / over die
Riviere Jeniscea / zijnse meest al te voet gheloopen / soo datter door onghemack veel sturven van de ghene die ghemac-
kelijck gheleeft hadden / ende vonden ten lesten even het selve
t'ghene de voorighe gheconfirmeert hadden: Boven dat soo
hoordense al te met ghelupdt van Volck ende Clocken / dan
haer vande Tingoesen ontraden zijnde / dorsten haer niet be-
gheven over dese Riviere / dan hebben in sommighe Bergen /
al-daer gheleghen / eenighe vlammen uyt sien springhen /
daer van sy eenich Solpher brochten / ende oock Goud-steen /
soo dattet schijnt / daer veel kostelijcke Mynen zijn mochten.

Den Gouverneur in Siberia liet oock eenighe schupten
toe maecken die berdeckt waren/en beval haer met het boo2-
jaer te baren tot Zee/upt de Kibiere Obp/ en gheboodt datse
langs de Zee-cant neffens landt souden baren/tot datse souden comen tot de Kibiere Jenistea/want hp sepde datse oock
moest endighen inde Zee / en beval haer daer in te repsen ce-
nige dach-repsen/daer teghens sandt hp oock bolck te lande/
bebelende haer soo langhe daer te blijben op de cant ban de
Kibiere / tot dat sp dese schupten bernemen souden / en gheboodt haer soo sp die niet en bernamen/na een jaer wederom
te keeren: Hebbende die ter Zee boeren bebolen / datse alles
souden besichtighen watter te sien ware/en gaf haer oock eenen Oversten met/die Luca ghenaemt was/ den welcken hp
beval/alles op te teeckenen/ en heeftse soo heenen ghesonden/
en sp zijn oock ghecomen inde mondt bande Kibiere boo2sz.
ende hebben malcanderen daer ontmoet/ alsoo die te Lande
waren ghetrocken / met den af-loop der Kibiere / op blotten
en schupten eenighe af-ghesonden hadden / die op den Zee-
cant de schupten ontmoeten/ ende bonden alles ghelijck den
Gouverneur haer te boo2en berhaelt hadde/teweten/ na sijn
mepninghe: Dan alsoo haren Overseen Luca boo2sz. ghe-
sto2ben was / met noch eenighe andere ban de boo2naemste/
hebbense gheraden ghebonden ban malcanderen te schepden/
ende elck weder sijns weeghs te trecken/ende zijn int wederom comen/ weder thups ghearribeert: in Siberia comende/
en alles op-geteeckent/ hebbense seer goet rappoo2t daer ban
aen den Gouverneur ghedaen/ die t'selbe aen den Kepser in
Mosco sondt/en is t'selbe ghesloten inde schat-camer in Mos-
co/so langhe tot dat dese Oo2loghen gheepndicht souden zijn/
alsdan soudet oversien wo2den/ maer denck het al berlo2en
is / d'welck jammer is / want sp beel seltsaems daer bonden
ban Eplanden ende Kibieren/ Boghels ende Dieren/ tot
boo2-bp de Jenistea heel wijt.
    Ende soo eenen goeden b2iendt in Moscobia daer eenen
b2oeder heenen gehadt hadde/ gaf mp een blinde Caerte daer
ban ghelijck hp't upt sijn b2oeders mondt berstaen hadde/die
doodt is / dan selber is hp doo2 Wapgats gheweest / ende
kent alle plaetsen tot Obp/dan wat daer boo2bp is / heeft hp
                                                    maer.

maer ghehoozt / soo en is t'selve Caertgen maer een bewerp
daer van neffens denZee-cant/d'welck ick met groote moeyte
te vercreegh / want dat het upt quame het soude dien Moscoviter synen hals costen/daerom laten hem onghenaemt.

Inde groote Riviere Oby comt oock een Riviere vallen
diese Caas noemen/ende schijnt te comen van ontrent Jenis-
cea/upt een groot Bosch/daer upt oock een Riviere valt/niet
wyt vande boozsz./die in Jeniscea valt/soo datse upt de Oby
te water comen reysen dooz de Samopedens Landouwe / en
setten haer maer twee mylen over Landt / soo comense in een
Riviere diese Cozgalf noemen / ende vallen soo met vallende
water in Jenistea / en t'selve is seer bequaem om repsen/
ende is ghebonden nu onlanghs van de Samopeden ende
Cingoesen.

Maer t'is jammer dat het den Hollanders niet en ghe-
luckt dooz Waygats te comen/doch en weten niet hoe sy t'selve souden te werck stellen/want met schepen/daer in hondert
mael niet dooz te comen en is : Maer alsse immers die Landen alle wilden doozspieden / moestense daer twee ofte dzie
faer blijben/omtrent Waygats oft Pechoza/daerse wel goede Haven ende lijf-tocht souden crygen/ ende van daer moeten sy volck senden met Booten/gelijck de Russen doen/ende
oock eenighe vziendtschap met den Russen maecken / die
haer dan geerne den wegh souden wijsen / ende alsoo soudet
ontdeckt werden.

Vele schoone plaetsen souden ondeckt wozden/ so van Eylanden als vast Landt / dan is aen te twijffelen of America
omtrent China niet aen dese dzie deelen des Werelts vast is
met een enghde ghelijck Africa aen Asia hanght / by de roode
Zee/ en t'selve is voozwaer wel moghelijck / want wie weet
te segghen oft open is / anders danse upt de sommighe schzif-
ten der Heydenen ghebonden hebben/ die schzyben dattet van
een gheschepden is/ende veel bewijs-redenen by bzenghen.

Oft soo het open is/so moet de strate seer enghe zyn/ want
ick by na ghesept hadde/dat het onmoghelijck soude zyn/ dat
de menschen in America souden comen / daer Adam in Asia
gheschapen is/ende daermen nerghens inde heylighe Schzif-
ten leest / dat booz de Dilubie eenighe Schepen of Schupten
                            D 3   waren/

waren / ende oock weet-men wel datter maer een Werelt en
is / eñ op geen diversche plaetsen schepselen haren oorspronck
en hebben / dan uyt den Paradyse / etc.

Nu mochtmen oock weder seggen / hoe de menschen alomme inde Eylanden ghecomen zijn / ende dit is / nae mijn meyninghe / nae de Diluvie gheschiet : Oock die in America / daer
is een enghe strate gelijckmen weet / ende sulcken engen strate mach tusschen Asia ende America oock wel zijn : hoe wel
uut sommige hart drijven / datter een groote Zee tusschen bey-
den is ober 100 mylen breedt.

F I N I S.

Verhael

Uan seker Memoziael/

ghepzesenteert aen zyne Majestept/

by den Capiteyn Pedro Fernandez de Quir ; aen=
gaende de bebolckinghe ende ontdeckinghe ban't bierde
deel des Werelts/ ghenaemt Austrialia incognita,
ofte onbekent Austrialia, zijn grooten rijck=
dom ende bzuchtbaerhept/ontdect
by den selben Capiteyn.

Heere,

Ck **Capiteyn** Pedro Fernandez de Quir,
segghe dat dit de achtste Requeste is die ick uwe
Majestept hebbe ghepresenteert / aengaende de bebolckinghe die daer behoozt te gheschieden in het
Landt dat uwe Majestept belast heeft t'ontdecken
in het quartier ban't onbekent Austrialia /sonder
datter tot noch toe resolutie met my ghenomen is/
noch eenighe antwoozd oft hope die my bersekere ban mijn af-beer=
dingh/ daer ick nochtans 14 maenden in dit Hof ben gheweest/ende
14 jaren dese sake ghehandelt heb sonder besoldinghe/ ende sonder
datter pet tot mynen boozdeele ghesloten is / maer alleen om haerder
goedhepd wille/met de welcke/ende met ontellicke tegenspzekinghen
ick 20000 mylen soo ter Zee als te Lande ghereyst ben/ende alle myne goederen berteert / ende mynen persoon ontrieft heb / lydende soo
bele ende soo schzickelicke dingen/dat sy my selbe ongheloofflick schy-
nen te zijn/alles om niet te berlaten een werck ban soo grooten God-
bzuchticheyd ende barmherticheyd. Ten welcken aensiene/ ende om
alle de Liefde Gods ick uwe Majestept wel ootmoedelick bidde/dat
sy niet ghedient en sy te ghedooghen/dat ick ban soo grooten ende soo
ghestadighen arbeyd ende onruste/ende ban een soo merckelick ende
wel ghefondeert aenhouden / niet en trecke de bzuchten daer ick soo
seer nae berlanghe ende pzetendere/ naedemael de eere ende glozie
Godes/ ende den dienst ban uwe Majestept/ daer so beel aen ghele=
ghen is/ende daer oneyndelijck beel goed upt spzupten sal/dat dueren
sal soo langh als de Wereld staet/ende hier nae inder eeuwichepd.

1. Aengaende de grootte ban dese nu nieuwelicx ontdeckte Lan=
den/oozdeelende nae't ghene dat ick ghésien heb/ende nae't ghene de
Capiteyn Louijs de Paez de Tozres/Admirael onder mijn ghebied/
uwe

uwe Majestept gheadbiseert ofte verwitticht heeft / soo is nae goede
reden haer lengde so groot als die ban gantsch Europa : Clepn Asia
tot aen de Caspische Zee toe / ende Persia / met alle de Eplanden ban
de Middellantsche ende groote Zee / omtrent ende rondtsom de selfde Provincien / Enghelandt ende Ierlandt mede daer in begrepen:
Dit berbozghen deel is t'bierde ban den gheheelen Aerdt-cloot / ende
soo groot dat daer in moghen zijn tweemael soo beel Coninckrijcken
ende heerlijckheden als alle de ghene daer ban uwe Majestept tegen-
woozdelick Heer is / ende dat sonder benabuert te zijn / met Turcken /
Mozen / ofte ander natien / die ghewoon zijn hare ghebueren te ont-
rusten ende te beroeren. Alle de Landen bp ons ghesien / liggen
binnen de Zona-tozrida / ende een deel ban dien raect tot den Equi-
noctiael die 90. Graden bzeedt moghen zijn / ende sommighe minder /
ende indien sp op-gaen na dat sp beloben / daer sullen Landen in ligghen teghen de boeten ban t'beste ban Africa ende heel Europa ende
t'meeste deel ban groot Asia.

   Ick waerschouw / dat nadien de Landen bp mp gesien op 15. Graden / beter zijn dan Spangien / dat de andere die in hoochte daer teghen ligghen naer addenant / moeten een Aerdtsch Paradijs zijn.

2.   In dese Landen is beel bolck / hare berwen zijn Wit / Bzupn /
Mulaetsch / Indiaensch / ende ghemenghelt / t'hapz hebben sp som
swazt / lang ende los / som ghefriseert ende ghekrolt / sommighe oock
rood ende seer dun / welcke berschepdenhept een teecken is ban groote
onderhandelinghen ende bp-eencomsten / om welcke reden / als mede
om de deucht des Landts / ende dooz dien sp gheen Gheschut oft ander Vper-werck en hebben om malcander te moozden / ende om dat
sp in gheen Silber-berghen en wercken / ende beel andere redenen /
het te ghelooben staet / dat dit bolck seer menichbuldich is / men can
niet mercken dat sp eenighe konst hebben t'zp clepn ofte groot / noch
mueren noch sterckten / noch Coninck noch Wet / ten zijn anders niet
ban een hoop slechte Hepdenen / ghedeelt in partpschappen ende geen
goede bzienden onder malcanderen / hare ozdinarise Wapenen zijn
bogen ende schichten / doch onbergift / knodsen / stocken / pijcken / ende
wozp-pijlen altesamen ban hout / sp decken hare schamelhepdt / zijn
pumich / bzolijck / redelijck / ende soo danckbaer als ick selfs bebon-
den hebbe / upt alle het welcke te hopen staet / dat sp met Godes booz-
sichtichepdt ende sachte middelen seer goedt te ghesegghen / te bebze-
dighen / te onderwijsen ende te bol-doen sullen zijn / het welcke dzie
saecken zijn inden aenbang seer noodich / om dese lupden altemale te
bzenghen tot die soo heplighe epnden / die men in't minst ende meest
met den besten pber ende ernst moet booz nemen : De hupsen zijnder
ban hout / ghedecht met bladeren ban palmboomen / sp ghebzupcken
aerde potten / hebben ghetouwen ghebzepdtsels ende ander ghebzep-
de Netten / sp bearbepden Warbersteen / maecken Flupten / Trom-
mels/

mels/ ende Lepels van hout al vernifcht/ fp hebben hare Ghebede:
huyfen ende begrabinghen/hare Hoven wel op-ghefchickt/ betupnt/
ende bepaelt/ fp behelpen haer veel met Parlamoer-fchelpen / ende
maecken daer af Gudtfen/Beptels/Foꝛmoirs/Saghen/Houwelen/
ende foo groote als clepne teecaenen die fp aenden hals dꝛaghen: De
Eplanders hebben hare Scheepkens wel ghewꝛacht/ende bequaem
om van t'een Landt in t'ander te varen/ het welck al te famen een
feecker teecken is van nabuerfchap/ met volck dat beter gepoliceert
is/eñ geen minder teecken van dien en is t'lubben van verckens e n-
de hoenderen.

3. Het bꝛoodt dat fp hebben/zijn dꝛie foozten van Woꝛtelen/die daer
in groote menichte zijn / ende comen dooꝛ fonder arbeydt/ want fp
daer toe niet anders en doen dan dat fp die bꝛaden ende koocken / fp
zijn fmaeckelijck ghefondt ende voedtfaem/dueren langhe/daer zijnder die een ellen langh ende een half elle dick zijn: De Frupten zijn
vele ende feer goedt / Platanos van fefterley aert/ groote menichte van
Amandelen van vierderley foozte/ groote Obos,dat een bꝛucht is van
groote ende fmaeck als Que-appels/veel iulandtfche Noten/ Oꝛan-
gien ende Limoenen die d'Indianen niet en eten/ende ander uptne-
mende ende groote Frupten/niet min goet/diemen ghefien ende ghe-
gheten heeft / met vele ende feer groote Supcker-rieten/ende kennis
van Appelen: Daer zijn ontallijck veel Palmboomen daer men ter-
ftondt Cuba upt trecken can / van de welcke men maeckt Wijn / E-
dick/Honigh ende Wep/ende de Palmitas zijn feer goedt/ de bꝛucht
die defe Palmboomen gheven/ zijn Cocos/ als fp groen zijn/ dienen
fp in plaetfe van Cardos/ ende het Mergh is als Room/ rijp zijnde/
ist onderhoudt van fpijs ende dꝛanck / ter Zee ende te Lande/ als fp
oudt zijn gheven fp Olp om te lichten/ende met te Meefteren als met
Balfem/ oock om t'eten /jong zijnde zijn de Schoꝛffen goede Vaten
ende Fleffen/ de binnenfte fchoꝛffen zijn werck om Schepen met te
Calfaten / ende alderley Cabels ende takel / oock oꝛdinaris touwen
ende Lonte van te maecken: Ende dat het befte is van de bladeren/
maecktmen feylen tot clepne Scheepkens/ ende fijne Matten/ ende
Tichelen daermen de huyfen met voert ende deckt/ welcke ghefpan-
nen werden met die ftammen die recht ende hooch zijn/eñ bande fel-
vige maecktmen Plancken/ Pijcken/ ende andere foozten van wape-
nen/ende Riemen/met veel andere goede dingen om dagelijcr te befi-
gen: Ende ftaet te bemercken dat defe Palmgaerden een Wijngaerd
zijn daer men t'heele jaer deur van pluckt ende Wijn van leeft / ende
nochtans niet van nood en heeft eenighe weldaed/coftende noch geld
noch tijd. De Moes-crupden diemen daer heeft ghefien zijn Ca-
woerden / groote ende vele Bledos ende groene Crupden: Men heefter oock Boonen vernomen. Belanghende t'Veefch/ daer zijn veel
Verckens tam als de onfe/ Hinnen/ Capoenen/ Patrpfen/ Epnt-bo:

ghels/Coꝛteldupben/Dupben/Waldupben ende Gepten/die den an=
deren Capitepn ghesien heeft. De Indianen hebben ons te ken=
nen ghegheben ban Koepen ende Buffels. De Disschen zijn bele/
Hargos, Pesce-reyes, Lizas, Conghen/ Salmkens/ Meros, Elst/ Macabis,
casanes, Pampanos, Sardpnen/Kocchen/Zeehanen/Chitas-viejas, Palin=
ghen/Pesces Puercos, Chapines, Rubia Almexas ende Garnet / ende ander
sooꝛten daer np de naem niet ban booꝛ en staet/ende daer moetender
noch beel meer zijn/naedemael alle de berhaelde t'samen ghebanghen
zijn dicht bp de schepen. Ende soo men t'ghene gheschꝛeben is wel
bemerckt/ men sal bebinden datmen ban soo bele ende soo goede lees=
tocht terstond ghenieten can groote ende bele lieffelijckheden /selfs
tot Marsepepnen ende beelderlepe Conserben toe/ende dat sonder pet
te bꝛenghen ban bupten: Ende ten aensiene ban't Boots-bolck / bo=
ben t'ghene berhaelt is/en sullender niet ontbꝛeken bele groote Ham=
men/potten met Boter/ende t'gene daer meer ban groote Berckens
af balt/sonder gebꝛeck ban Suer ende Specerien / staet aen te merc=
ken dat bele ban de booꝛsz.dinghen de onse ghelijck zijn / ende datter
moghelijck beel meer zijn/ ende dat het Land hier dooꝛ toont seer be=
quaem te zijn om booꝛt te bꝛenghen alle ander dinghen diemen bint
in Europa.

4. De Rijckdommen zijn Silber ende Peerlen/die ick/en Goud/
dat den anderen Capitepn ghesien heeft/soo hp seght/in zijn bertoog/
t'welck de dꝛie rijcxste sooꝛten zijn die de nature gheschapen heest.
Daer is beel Note Moscaet/Mastick/Peper/Gengber/ dat wp bep=
de gesien hebben. Men heefter wetenschap ban Caneel/t'mach oock
wel datter Naghelen zijn/naedemael de andere Specerien daer zijn/
ende te meer om dat die Landen parallel zijn/ oft wepnich berschil=
len ban Terrenate ende Bachan. Daer is oock stoffe om Spde te
winnen/Pita, Supcker/Anir te maecken. Daer is goet Ebbenhout/
ende ontallicke sooꝛten ban Hout/om soo beel Schepen te maken als
men wilt/met alle haere Seplen/ ende dꝛiederlep sooꝛten ban Takel/
t'een ghelijckende onsen Kennip/ende met de Olie ban Cocos canmen
Galagala maken/daer men Teer mede berspaert. Daer is seker Ter=
pentijn gesien daer sich de Indianen met behelpen om hare Piraguas,
ofte Schepen/ te peken. Ende naedemael datter Gepten zijn / ende
kennis ban Koepen/soo salder oock Coꝛduaen/Leer/Roet en Bleesch
oberbloedich zijn : Ende Bpen ghesien zijnde / salder oock Honich
ende Was zijn. Ende behalben alle dese rijckdommen bersekeren sp
ban beel andere kenischappen. Ende de ghelegenthept ende gestal=
tenisse des Lands/ de welcke gheboecht zijnde bp de bele die de neer=
stichepd geben sal/naedien daer soo grooten booꝛraed is ban haer ep=
ghen dinghen/ende om de onse te queken / die ick booꝛ heb daer met
den eersten te boeren / met noch alle de andere beste ende nutste die in
Peru ende nicu Spaengien groepen/schijnt het dat dit al t'samen bp
een

een ghevoecht/het Land soo rijck sal maken/dat het genoechsaem sal
zijn om beyde hem selven ende America te voeden / ende Spaengien
groot ende rijck te maken/in sulcker voeghen als ick betoonen sal/in=
dien ick by andere gheholpen werd om dit upt te voeren. Ende ten
aensien van't ghene ghesien is/wesende Zee-custen/seg ick/Heere/dat
upt het hert van't Land te verhopen zijn soo groote ende soodanighe
grootheden ende rijckdommen/ende goede saken / als de onse begin=
nen te werden. Staet te noteren dat mijn principael voornemen al=
leen is gheweest te soecken so grooten Land als ick ghebonden hebbe/
ende dat ick om myne crancten ende ander oorsaken/ die ick verswy=
ge/niet en heb connen so veel sien als ick gewilt heb/ oock en conde al
t'gene ick begeerde/niet gesien werden in een maend/daer-der twaelf
van in een Jaer comt/de welcke te kennen gheven de qualiteyten en=
de vruchten die alle de gheschapene Landen voortbrenghen/ende dat
men de Indianen van die Landen niet en moet oordeelen upt onse
behoeftigheden/smaken/begeerlickheden ende achtinghe van saken;
maer voor menschen die haer leven trachten over te brenghen met so
weynich arbeyds als sy connen/ ghelijck sy oock doen / sonder haer te
vermoeyen in yet meer/daer wy ons om vermoeyen.

5. De gherieflickheyd ende het ghenoechlicke leven sal daer soo
groot zijn als men siet/in een soo gheoeffenden/lustighen ende koelen
Land/dat swart/vet ende goed van Meyn is/met Leem-putten/om
terstond Huysen te moghen bouwen ; Steen/ Ticchelen/ ende al wat
meer van Leem wert ghemaeckt/ oock met vele ende soo nae by ghe=
leghen rouwe ende viercante Marbersteenen/ om costelicke en̅ schoo=
ne Ghebouwen te moghen stichten : Soo veel ende soo dienstelicken
Hout tot alle noodighe wercken;sulcken gheleghentheyd van Dalen/
Velden/den meestendeel door-ghesneden / ende hooghe dubbele Rot=
sen/ sulcke Beerxkens ende vlietende Rivieren/ daer bequamelijck
connen Water-molens/Azeñas, Trapiches ende ander Water-wercken
ghemaeckt worden. Essenos, Sout-pannen ende Riet-bosschen ghe=
tuyghen van de vruchtbaerheyd des Lands / daer men Rieten bindt
van vijf ende ses palmen / ende min / ende de vrucht naer advenant/
t'eynd dun ende hart/de huyt glat/ ende soo goede Ypersteenen alsser
zijn in Madrid.

De Baye van Sint Philips ende Jacob heeft twintich mylen
strands/sy is gheheel schoon/ ende bry om in te comen by daghe ende
by nachte/heeft rond-om veel bewoonde Vlecken/ in de welcke(ende
dat seer verre)men by daghe veel roocks sach opgaen/ ende by nach=
te veel vyers/hare haben ghenaemt Veracruz / het ware kruys is so
ruym datter meer dan duysent schepen in moghen ligghen/de grond
is schoon ende van swart zandt / men heefter gheen buylen ghesien/
men can daer setten op soo veel Vadem als men wilt / van veertich
tot een half toe/tusschen twee Rivieren/de een soo groot als de Gua=

C 2   dalquevir

dalquebir in Sebilien/met een Barre oft ſtoztende bloedt/ ban meer
als twee badem/ daer goede Fregatten ende Pataſſen in moghen/in
d'ander boeren onſe Barcken bzp in / ende ſchiepen daer water dat
ſeer ſchoon is op alle de plaetſen/ban de bele daermen het bindt: De
Loſ-plaets is een ſtrand ban dzie mijlen/ ende meeſt al keſelachtich/
ban ſwarte/clepne ende ſware kepen/ſeer goedt om Schepen te bal-
laſten/de ſtrand/dooz dien ſp geen bzeucken oft kreken heeft/ende om
dat de krupden op de tant groepende/groen zijn/wierdt berſtaen niet
gheſlaghen te werden bande Zee / ende alſoo de boomen aldaer al te
mael recht op ſtonden/ſonder ſchade nochte bederf/ ſo oozdeelde men
daer upt datter gheen groote onwederen en moeſten ballen: Deſe ha-
ben/ boben dat ſp ſoo luchtich is / heeft een ander groote uptnement-
hept/ten aenſie ban bermakelijckhept/want ſo haeft als den dach aen
quam/ hoozdemen dooz t'gheheele naebp-ghelegben Boſch een ſeer
ſoete Harmonpe ban menich dupſent berſchepden bogbelen / ſommi-
ghe(ſoo't ſcheen)Nachtegalen/ſommige Meerlen/ Quacken/ Diſtel-
bincken/ontellijcke Swaluwen/Periquitos,ende een Papegap die men
ſach/ende behalben deſe beel ander ſoozten ban bogbelen/ſelfs tot het
ſinghen bande Spzinck-hanen ende Krekels/heele mozghenſtonden
ende abonden langh roockmen beel ſoete reucken/her romende ban ſo
beelderlep aert ban bloemen /tot Ozangien bloepſels ende t'crupdt
Alvahaca : Ende om alle deſe ende andere goede ſaecken beſloot men
dat het daer moeſt goede Lucht zijn / ende datter de natuere haer oz-
dze wel onderhieldt.

6. Deſe haben ende hare Bape werden noch uptnemender dooz de
nabuerſchap ban ſo beel goede Eplanden / ende ſonderlinghe ban ſe-
ben/daer den roep af is datſe twee hondert mijlen groot zijn/het eene
begrijpter bijſtich/ende lep[t]er twaelf ban berſchepden : In ſomma
ick ſegh Heere dat op deſe Bap ende Haben/die 15.¼.Gzaden hoochte ban de noozder Pool ligghen/terſtont can geſticht werden een ſeer
groote ende bolckrijcke Stadt/ende dat de lupden die deſelbe bewoo-
nen/ſullen ghenieten alle ghewenſche rijckdommen ende gherieflic-
heden/ die den tijdt ſal leeren/ ende die men mach medebeelen aen de
Pzobincien ban Chili/Peru/Panama/Nicaragua/Gatemale/nieu
Spaengien/ Terratena ende Filippinas/ ban alle welcke Landen
uwe Majeſtept Heer is / ende indien uwe Majeſtept oock Heer wozd
ban deſe die ick pzeſentere/ſo houd ickſe ban ſulcker weerde/ dat/bo-
ben dien dat ſp ghelijck als de ſleutels zijn ban de booz-berhaelde/ ſp
(nae ick berſtae) ſullen comen te weſen/ ſoo beel den handel belangbt
ban curicuſe ende pzofijtelijcke Waren/ Heerlickhepdt laet ick ſtaen/
zen tweede China/Japan/ende andere pzobincien op die kuſten ban
Aſia met hare Eplanden/ende ick balle cozt na t'gheen ick daer ban
gheboele/ende in een bergaderingh ban Wiſ-conſtenaers can bewij-
ſen/oock en berleng ick mp hier niet met te ſeggen/ dat deſe Landen
terſtont

terſtondt connen helpen/ ende onderhouden/ twee hondert dupſendt
Spaengaerden: In ſomma Heere dit is de werelt daer Spaengien
het middel-punt ban gaet wozden/ende ten aenſien ban t'lichaem is
dit de naghel/datmen bzy dit punt wel noteere.

De ghetemperthepdt/ende deucht des Luchts/Heer/is ſoodanich
als men upt alle t'ghene boozſept is/ſien can/ ende oock hier aen
bemercken mach/dat alhoewel de onſe daer alle bzeemdelingen wa-
ren/ niemandt nochtans en is ſieck ghewozden/niet teghenſtaende
het ozdinaris wercken/ſweeten/ende nat wozden/ſonder ſick te ont-
houden ban water te dzincken noch nuchter zijnde/oft ban alles te
eten dat het landt boozbzenght/noch ban den abondtſtondt/Maen/
ofte Son/ die by daghe niet ſeer bzandich en was: Ende achter de
middernacht epſchte ende conde men ſeer wel berdzaghen een wol-
len decxel: Ende naedien de inlanders in't ghemepn bolhbich ende
ſeer bzoom zijn/ſommighe oock ſeer oudt/ daer ſp nochtans neben
der Aerde woonen/ t'welck een groot teecken is ban goeder gheſont-
hepdt/ want ware t'Landt ongheſondt/ ſp ſouden hare hupſen ban
der Aerde berheffen/ ſoo men in de Filippinen doet/ende in ander
quartieren die ick gheſien hebbe/ nadien oock de biſch ende t'bleeſch
ongheſouten zijnde/ twee daghen ende langher goet bleben/naedien
de Frupten ban daer ghebzacht/ſoo men ſien mach/ aen twee die ick
hier hebbe/ſeer geſont zijn/ alhoewel ſp bupten tijts ban de boomen
ghepluckt zijn/nadien men daer geene ſandige gronden en heeft ge-
ſien/ noch gheenderlep diſtelen oft dooznachtige boomen/oock ghee-
ne boomen die hare woztelen boben der Aerde hebben/ noch eenighe
berdzoncken belden/ noch Poelen/ noch Sneeu op de hooghe Ber-
ghen/noch Cocodzillen in die Ridieren/ noch benynighe quaedtaer-
dighe ghewozmte op t'gheberchte/ noch Mieren die ghemepnlijck
in de hupſen ende bzuchten ſeer ſchadelijck zijn/ noch Niguas, noch
Rupſen/noch Mugghen/ ſoo ſeggh' ick/ dat dit tot ons booznemen/
een uptnementhepdt is boben alle uptnementheden/ ende weerdigh
geacht te zijn ſo ſeer als bele Landen in de Indien/ die om deſe ple-
ghen alleen onbewoonbaer te zijn/ ende andere/ daermen ſo beel ban
deſelbe te lijden heeft/als ick wel ghetupghen can.

7.   Dit zijn Heere de uptnementheden ende deuchd der Landen
die ick ontdeckt heb/ ban de welcke ick upt den naem ban uwe Majeſtept de poſſeſſie ghenomen heb/onder uwen Koninghlicken Stan-
daert/ende alſoo ghetupghen't de acten die ick hier hebbe.

Ten eerſten/Heere/wierter een Cruys opgherecht/ende een Kerck
toeghemaeckt ban onſe Vzouw' ban Lozeto/ daer wierden twintich
Miſſen ghedaen/ men berdiendet den Aflaet op den Pincxterdach
                              C 3   berleent/

verleent/ende daer wiert een solemnele processie ghehonden op't Sacraments dach. In somma het alderheplichste Sacrament/hebbende uwer Majestepts Standaert tot Lepds-man / bewandelde ende vereerde die verborgen Landen/daer ick drie Veld-banieren op hebbe gherecht/ende in alle de selve vertoont de twee Colomnen ter zpde van uwe Coninghlijcke Wapenen: Waer door ick met recht seggghen mach/voor so veel dit een deel is/ dat hier is volbracht het woord van Plus ultra, ende voor so veel het vast Land is al border ende achterder. Ende dit / met al watter meer ghedaen wierdt / heb ick ghedaen als een ghetrouw' Vassael/soo ick ben van uwe Majestept/ende ten epnde uwe Majestept dit terstond moghe bp-boeghen/op dat clincke den heerlijcken titel van Austrialia van den Hepligen Gheest/tot meerder eere van den selfden Heere/ die mp ghelept/ het Land ghetoont/ ende in teghenwoordichepd van uwe Majestept ghebracht heeft / al-waer ick stae met den selven wille/die ick altijt tot dese sake ghehadt hebbe/ die ick hebbe ghequeeckt/ende om hare weerdichepd ende verdienste boben maten lief heb ende toeghedaen ben.

Ick gheloobe wel/ upt den wpsen Raed/ Grootmoedichepd/ ende Christelicke Godbruchtichepd van uwe Majestept/ de groote sorghe die sp draghen sal om sos berseeckert te zijn van de bebolckinghe deser alreets ontdeckte Landen/ als wel behoort/aenghesien de principael oorsaeck die ons behoort te verbinden/om de selfde niet woest ende onbewoont te laten/is/dat dit de remedie is/dienende te epnde dat God onse Heere daer in werde ghekent/ ghelooft/ aenghebeden ende ghedient/ daer nu de Dupbel soo seer ghedient werd: Te meer oock dat dit de deure sal zijn/ waer door aen so bele Volckeren/staende onder't ghebiedt van uwe Majestept/ incomen sal alle haer goed ende welbaerd /ende de ongheljck meerder sorghen die boortcomen souden/ bp aldien daer heenen geraeckten te gaen de bpanden van de Roomsche Kercke / om hare balsche leeringhen te berbzepden / ende alle de goederen die ick te kennen ghebe te beranderen in meerder quaden/ ende sich te noemen Heeren van Indien / ende die heel te verderben. Oock gheloof ick dat uwe Majestept wel berwitticht is dat soo swaren schade/als die is daer ban ghesproken werdt/oft alderlep andere ongheschickthept/die nu boorhanden is/of naemaels soude moghen wesen / costen soude millioenen Gouds ende beel dupsend menschen/ eer men soude tot een onseker remedie connen comen: Vwe Majestept winne nu/nadiē sp't bermach/met wepnich silbers in Peru upt-gheghehen/om eenmael den Hemel te winnen/ den eeuwigen naem/ ende de nieuwe Werelt/met al t'ghene sp toesepdt: Ende naedemael daer niemant is die uwe Majestept boden-brood epscht ban so grooten ende merckelijcken weldaedt Godes / voor uwen gheluckighen tijdt bewaert/so epsch ick boden-brood Heere/ende in plaets van dien mijn afberdingh ende beschepdt/want de Galeoenen zijn reed/ende ick

ick heb veel te repsen/ ende toe te maecken / ende veel te beschicken/ oock is het geestelijck ende tijdelijck goedt seer veele dat alle uere ber= lozen gaet/ende nimmermeer weder en can bercreghen wozden.

Hebben Chzistoffel Colon sijne suspicien hartneckich ghemaeckt/ t'ghene mp soo moeplijck doet vallen /is dat ick selve gesien ende ge= tast heb / ende nu aenbiede. Waer toe uwe Majestept gheliebe / dat van soo veel remedien alsser zijn / daer een alleen werde ghegheben/ op dat ick t'boozghestelde erlanghen mach / waerschouwende dat men mp in alles seer redelick sal bevinden / ende ick sal in alles vol= noegingh gheben.

Heere / dit is een groot werck / naedemael de Duybel het selve soo bloedigen krijch aen doet/ende t'en is niet wel dat hp so veel vermach wesende uwen Majestept daer van den bescherm-Heer.

FINIS.

Verhael vande Reyse/
ende de Nieuw-ghevonden Strate
van Mr Hudson.

MR. Hudson die ettelijcke malen Weſtwaerts een dooꝛgangh gheſocht heeft/ had zijn ooghmerck om dooꝛ Lumbleps inlet in Fretum Davis in een dooꝛgaende Zee te comen/ ghelijck wp ſulcꝛ in zijn Caerte bp Mr Plantius geſien hebben/ en bp weſten Noba Albion in Mar del Zur te loopē/daer een Enghels-man/ ſoo hp gheteeckent had/ dooꝛ ghepaſſeert was. Maer nae veel moeptens heeft hp deſe wech/die hier op dees Caerte gheteeckent ſtaet/gevonden/ die hp vervolcht ſoude hebben/ hadde't ghemeen Scheeps-volck niet ſoo onwillich gheweeſt: want alſo ſp wel 10 maendē uptgeweeſt hadden/daerſe nochtans maer vooꝛ 8 maenden gevict alieert waren/ ende op de heele wech maer een man gheſien hebben/die haer een groot Dier bꝛocht dat ſp aten; die/ om dat hp qualijck ghetracteert wiert/niet weer en quam/ſoo iſſet gemeen Scheeps-volck(als ſp weder vande hooꝛhte van 52 gr. daer ſp verwinterden/ tot op de hoochte van 63 grad. langhs de Weſt-zpde vande Bape/daer ſp in geloopen waren) op-gheclommen/daer ſp een rupme Zee ende groote baren upten Nooꝛdweſten vernamen/ endelick
teghens

tegens haer Meesters op-gestaen/die voorder voort wil
den/ende hebben d'Overhept altesamen in een Sloep
ófte schupt buyten scheeps gheset / ende zijn alsoo met
het Schip nae Enggelant geseylt : Hierom zijn sy/ als
sy t'huys quamen/altesamen in prison gheset/ende dese Somer zijnder op nieus schepē ter ordonnantie van
den Coningh ende den Prince van Wallis derwaerts
ghesonden/om de doorgangh verder t'ontdecken/ ende
Mr. Hudson met den zynen op te soecken : welcke schepen bevel hebben om met hun tween / als de passagie
ghevonden sal zijn/door te passeren/ ende een t'huys te
senden met de tydinghe/die wy verwachten.

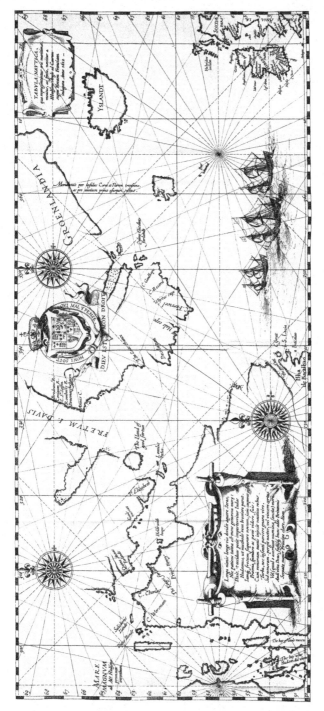

The material originally positioned here is too large for reproduction in this reissue. A PDF can be downloaded from the web address given on page iv of this book, by clicking on 'Resources Available'.

Aenmerckinghen op dese

Russche Caerte ende oock op de tusschen-reden die Isaac Massa by de beschrijvinghe ghevoecht heeft.

OP de Caerte heeft Massa de Russche naem / die met Griecksche Letteren gheschreven stondt / op't Landt daer boven de Strate Matseioftsar / anders Matenskinsarck ende Costinsarck genoemt / geinterpreteert voor America / ghelijck hy dat in mijn voorbeeldt gheschreven had / dat wel een groote faute is; want t'Landt dat Willem Barentsz. langhs gheseylt heeft / ende daer hy t'behouden huys op timmerde / streckt noch wel 60 mylen inde hoochte Noordelijcker; ende is ooc altoos met de naem Noba Semla ghenoemt / dat soo veel te segghen is / als Nieu-landt / dat men meent een Eylandt te wesen.

Van D. Peter Plantius heeft daer een tegen-meeninghe af / uyt het relaes van Willem Barentsz. ende Hans van Ysselen van Rotterdam / die hem vertelt hebbē verstaen te hebben uyt een Overste vande Samopeden aen de Zuyd-zyde vande Strate vā Weygats / dattet voornoemde Noba Semla Oostwaerts aen't Zuyder vaste Land vast is / ende dat de Mar More (dat hy nytleydt voor de stille Zee) Oostwaerts vol ijs verstopt leyt / dat uyt de groote Rivieren comt / t'welc uyt dese Caerte wel also eenichsins soude schynnen / waer't dat t'Land dat by Noorden de Riviere Peisida gheteeckent is / ende t'Land van noba Sembla aen een ghetrocken waer.

Van alsoo Jan Huyghen schrijft dat d'Amsterdammer Tolck veel dinghen qualijck verstaen heeft: ende dat de Russen aen zijn Tolck / Fransops de la Dale / ghesept hebben / dat men 100 f 20 mylen door de Straete van Weygats gantsch gheen ijs en vint; soo laten wy dese sake / als noch onseker zijnde / in twyfel hanghen.

Op

Op d'eerſte aen-ghetekende plaetſe daer Maſſa ſeydt dat hp bewyſen wil datmen niet door Weygats en mach/ ſtaet te mercken dat hp wat rondelijck de ſake af-ſept : want t'is immers van d'Enchupſers gedaen/en daerom ſout oock noch weer connen ghedaen worden; doch t'is blijckelijck dat-men't alle Jaren niet ſoude connen doen.

Ende in de tweede aen-gheteeckende plaetſe ſept hp/dattet in hondert Jaeren niet eens te doen is ; daer't nochtans van de drie malen dattet by onſe Hollanders beproeft is/eens ge-beurt is ende de tweede-mael warenſe oock al tot het Staten Eplandt ghecomen / van daer ſp upt vreeſe van in't ijs beſet te worden/zijn weder-ghekeert.

Ende de twpfelingen bande Strate van Anian/ſo men die gemeenlijck noemt/beſchrijft hp al wat ſlechtelijck/want hp fondeert zijn twpſel daer op/dat hp niet en weet hoe de men-ſchen in America ſouden ghecomen zijn/ ſoo'er een wpde tuſ-ſchen t vaſte Land van Aſia ende America ware ; daer noch-tans ſo wel de Chineſen en Japoneſen ten Weſten van haer; als onſe natie ten Ooſten van haer/ alle beyde van over lan-ghe eeuwen altoos ſchepen ghehadt hebben/daer met ſp licht connen derwaert overgheſet weſen.

Dit moet ick noch noteren / dat ick van't ongheluck van d'Amersfoorder Commijs aē nova Francia al veel te ſtijf in de Voor-reden gheſproken heb / want een ſacck is dickwils heel anders dan t hem ten eerſten laet acnſien / ende om dat ons d'oorſaccken daerom eenich diingh toeromt/ meeſt altijdt onbekent zijn / ſoo canmen ſulcke dinghen geenſins vaſt ſeg-ghen.

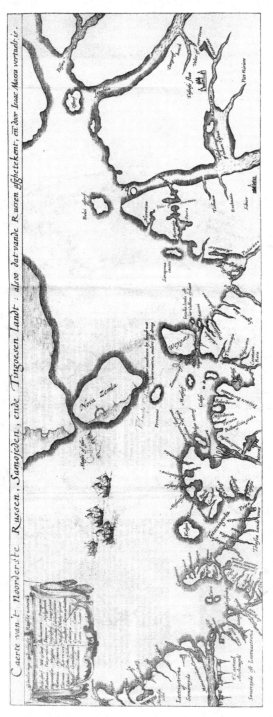

The material originally positioned here is too large for reproduction in this reissue. A PDF can be downloaded from the web address given on page iv of this book, by clicking on 'Resources Available'.

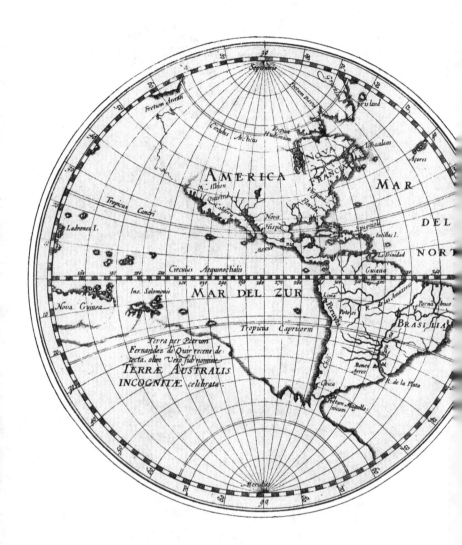

Descriptio ac delineatio Geographica

DETECTIO-
NIS FRETI

Sive, Tranfitus ad Occafum fuprà
terras Americanas, in Chinam
atq; Iaponem ducturi.

Recens investigati ab M. Henrico Hudfono Anglo.

Item,

Exegefis REGI HISPANIÆ facta, fuper
tractu recens detecto, in quintâ Orbis parte, cui nomen
AVSTRALIS INCOGNITA.

Cum defcriptione

Terrarum *Samoiedarum,* & *Tingoefiorum,* in
Tartariâ ad Ortum Freti VVaygats fitarum, nuperq;
fceptro Mofcovitarum adfcitarum.

AMSTERODAMI

Ex Officina Heffelij Gerardi. Anno 1613.

Liber ad Lectorum.

Qui cupis ignotas Lector cognoscere terras,
   Corpore quas fulgens contegit Vrsa suo,
Et simul extremos Boreæ, Cauriq; recessus,
   Et freta iam nautis per via fluctivagis.
Quasq; Samojedus commutet vellere merces,
   Quam latè Moschus proferat Imperium.
Impiger Hudsonius freta quæ petretraverit, & quæ
   Restat adhuc Batavis gloria Martigenis.
Me pretio parvo redimas, animoq; revolvas,
   Sim licet exiguus commoda magna feram.

Ad Lectorem Prolegomena,

in tractatus sequentes.

T antehac novæ terrarum detectiones, laboriosissimæque navigationes, tam Hispanorum, quam Anglorum, nec non Batavorum, maximo novitatem studioforum oblectamine, in lucem editæ fuere: Non alienum a publico commodo duxi, in Theatrum orbis hāc tabulam Præfecti H. Hudsonis producere de navigatione ipsius supra Americam, in Chinam, & Iapan: maximè cum viderem eam à præftantissimis viris magnoperè expeti: Ne autem ob brevitatem, exiguitatemque apud nonnullos vilesceret opusculum hoc adjunxi historiam Ducis Petri Fernandez de Queiros, quam in libello supplici Regi Hispaniæ exhibito, narrat de regionibus Meridionalibus, detectis in mari del Zur; eam nonnulli magni fecerunt, aliqui quibus de certitudine rei constat, veram esse asserunt. Octavius Pisanus, in suâ totius Orbis tabulâ, quam inverfâ delineatione, circulo comprehendit, de Regionibus à Petro Fernandez de Queiros detectis, delineationem suam se cōparasse ait, à Nauclero quodam, statuitque eas à parte occidentali, limæ, cidado de los reyos in Peru. Viginti quinque gradus in longitudinem, qui superant trecenta, & quinquaginta miliaria Germanica, extenditurque secundum illius delineationem, plusquam quingenta miliaria Germanica occidentem versus, at versus Meridiem extenditur usque à Doctissimo gradum ab Æquatore. Sed cum superiori Anno ab Illustri Viro Emanuele à figueiredo, Geographiæ, & Hydrographiæ Professore Vlixbonæ, nunciatum esset, Petrum Fernandez à Queiros nihil Geographiæ dignum prodidisse, sibiq; relationem tantum obscuram delatam esse, situ, latitudine regionum carentem: insuper hoc adderet, se diligentius inquæsiturum, num quid apud

eum

eum effet, quod ufui effe poffit; & adhuc eum effe in Curiâ vel Aulâ Regiâ Madritij, nec quid certi de profectione ejus ftatutum effe; Exemplar Octavij, Pifani fecutus non fum, maximè cum hic ex amicis quidam, affirmet apud fe effe delineationem Regionem, aut Infularum nouiter detectarum in Mari del Zur, quam brevi impetrabibus, eamq; cum Octavij Pifani delineatione conferemus. Cum vero apud Batavos ferbuerit aliquandiu ftudium inveftigandi tranfitum, in Chinam & Iaponiam, eumque tentarint non nulli Septemtrionem verfus, non nulli per VVeygats & mare Tartaricum, operæ pretium duxi, in publicum proferre, quæ à Ruffis proxima loca incolentibus detecta funt, Tabulâ ab Ifaaco Maffâ ex Idiomate Rufforum tranflata, ut quid de oris Samojedarum fit fentiendum certo conftet. Affiduæ etiam navigationes Cantabrorum, Batavorum, Anglorum in Septentrionum, venatione balænarium, & cuniculorum marinorum, gaudentium, quos Morfas idiomate proprio Ruffi nominant videntur quid certi promittere, de oris Novæ Semlæ, Nieulandiæ, ufq; ad Groenlandiam adhuc incognitis, fed de futuris contingentibus non eft determinata veritàs.

Defcriptio, ac delineatio Geographica
DETECTIONIS FRETI.

Sive tranſitus, ſupra terras Americanas
in Chinam, & Iaponem.

Elicifsimæ Anglorum navigationes, & proſperrimi earum ſucceſſus, magis ac magis iſti genti ſtimulum addiderunt, ut facile omnia tædia devorarint & novas deteċtiones ſuſceperint, quæ licet laborioſiſſimæ fuerint in Orientem ad ora Moſcoviæ, Novæ Zemlæ & Groenlandiæ, nihilominus deſudarũt in partibus Occidentalibus (occupatâ iam etiam illic, & colonijs ſuis infeſſa Virginia) ut ſibi tranſitum, intra Groenlandiam, & Novam Franciam quærerent ſed fruſtrâ haċtenus, ſeduċti viâ in Septemtrionem obduċtâ nivibus & glacie, elaboratum eſt, uſque ad altitudinem ſeptuaginta, aut oċtaginta graduum, nomenque traxit Fretum ab inventore primo Ioanne Davis, poſtremus qui idem iter inſtituit, præfeċtus fuit Georgius VVeymouth, qui anno milleſimo ſexcenteſimo ſecundo quingentas leucas navigando emenſus eſt, ſed glaciei copiâ coaċtus eſt, ut & alij anteceſſores, in patriam redire. Sed ne irritus plane eſſet conatus, navigans denuo, ad altitudinem, ſexaginta, & unius gradus, per ſinum quem Angli Lumles Inlet dicunt, ibi ob occidente in meridiem defleċtens centum leucas, poſtea objectu terræ, tranſitum non inveniens, imbecillitate ſociorum, alijſque de cauſis, coaċtus eſt reverti nihilominus & duos alios ſinus luſtravit, non ſine maxima aquarum copia maris inſtar, & maximo fluxu & refluxu, intra terram hanc, & eam quam Baccalaos apellant.

Hæc

Defcriptio detectionis Freti.

Hæc navigatio licet tum temporis, votis, non refponderit, tamen Diaria Georgij Weymouth (quæ inciderunt in manus D. P. Plantij, curiofiffimi rerum novarum inveftigatoris, in ufum patriæ hujus noftræ, reique Nauticæ) ufui fuerunt maximo, H. Hudfoni, in inveftigatione hujus famofiffimi Freti, cum enim anno millefimo fexcentefimo, & nono, ille ageret cum Præfectis Indicæ navigationis, de via inquirenda in Chinam & Catahayam, fupra Novam Zemlam, hæc à D. P. Plantio impetravit Diaria, ex quibus totū iftud iter Georgij Weymouth per anguftias fupra Virginiam didicit, ufque ad Oceanum, qui eam alluit, hinc ifta opinio invaluit, hac viâ folâ patere aditum ad Indos; fed quam vallax fit, docuit illum D. P. Plantius, ex relatu cujufdam, qui in parte Occidentali, terram effe continentem affeverarat, eamque luftrarat. Hudfonus nihilominus in Oriente, & Novâ Zemlâ, viam fibi à glacie, nivibus, præclufam videns, in Occidentem navigavit, ut quid fpeï fupereffet inquireret; non recto itinere (ut hic fertur) ut patriæ huic nostræ, & Præfectis prodeffet, tantum in Novâ Franciâ mercibus fuis commutatis, pro pellibus, falvus in Angliam reverfus eft, ibique accufatus in detrimentum Patriæ Angliæ navigationes fuas inftituiffe; Iterum iter fufcepit, non minori ftudio de tranfitu inveftigando in Occidente, tendens in Fretum Davis, anno millefimo fexcentefimo et decimo, ufq; ad altitudinem unjus & fexaginta graduum, ingreffus femitam Georgij VVeymouth, omnes oras luftravit, hac in tabulâ delineatas, ufque ad gradus fexagintà tres, deflexit in Meridiem ufq; ad gradus quinquaginta quatuor, fub ijs hybernavit, folvens iftinc littus Occidentale legēs, afcendit ufq; ad gradum fexagefimū, recta navigans quadraginta leucas, amplū pelagus deprehēdit, fluctibus à Cauro agitatis fuperbiens: Ex his non exigua fpes tranfeundi Hudfono affulfit, nec voluntas Senatui nautico defuit, fed faftidium, & malevolentia fociorum fcrupulum injecere, ob victus inopiam, cum ijs tātum in octo

menfes

Defcriptio detectionis Freti.

menfes prospectum effet, nihilque toto itinere alimento dignum in manus eorum incideret, nifi fortè Indus quidam, qui Criffio Mexicano, feu Iaponenfi armatus, feram attulit, ex quo Hudfonus conijciebat, fe non longè a Mexicanis abeffe, quorum arma, & commercia videret, Tādem prævaluit fociorum malevolentia, qui Hudfonum, cum reliqui præfectis fcaphâ expofuerunt in mare, ipfi patriam petiere, quam cum appuliffent, ab fcelus commiffum in carceres detrufi funt, ibiq; detinentur, donec Præfectus eorum Hudfonus falvus fuis reftituatur, ab ijs, quibus id negotij fuperiori anno millefimo, fexcentefimo, & duodecimo, juffu Principes VValliæ piæ memoriæ, & Præfectorum Ruffiæ navigationis commiffum eft, de quorum reditu hactenus nihil inauditum, hinc fpes aliqua affulget, eos anguftias illas fuperaffe nec judicamus quid certi nos inaudituros priufquam ex Indiâ Orientali redierint, aut ubi cum Chinenfibus, aut Iaponēfibus fua tranfegerint, eademque viâ in Angliam redierint: quod felix & fauftum fit precamur unicè.

Nec fervor ifte in noftris Amfterodamenfibus deferbuit planè, fuperioribus enim menfibus ab ijs emiffa eft navis, eo tantum fine, ut de tranfitu, vel Freto Hudfoni inquireret, & num commercij locus fit in iftis oris, fi vero eventus votis non refpondeat, in Oris Novæ Franciæ negotiabuntur.

Libelli fupplicis, oblati Regiæ Majeftati

Hifpaniæ, a Duce Petro Fernandez de Quir,

Super

Detectione quartæ partis Orbis terrarum, cui
nomen Auftralis incognita, eiusq; immenfis opibus
& fertilitate.

 Lluftriffime Rex, Octavum hunc libellum fupplicem tibi offero, fuper deductione coloniarum, in terras quas Majeftati Regiæ placuit detegi, in regione Auftrali incognitâ, ut hactenus in negotio eo nihil actum fit, nihilque refponfi aut fpei datum de felicifsimo eventu. Elapfi enim quatuordecim menfes, ex quo in Aulâ hîc fui, totidemque anni cum primum hæc agreffus fum, fine ullo ftipendio aut mercede, inductus folummodo præftantiâ Rei, devoratifque omnibus tædijs, viginti millibus leucis emēfis, terrâ ac mari, omnibus meis abfumptis, mihi ipfi defuiffe videor, tanta, tamque horrenda paffus, ut vix effari liceat, eo fine ut pium hoc, & laudabile opus abfolverem.

Quare ad pedes Regiæ Majeftatis fupplex me devolvo, ne præmijs juftis & debitis continuis laboribus, & moleftijs meis defrauder: Cum fciam quanti interfit divinæ gloriæ. Regiæ Majeftati, nec exigua hæc paritura commoda non tantum his feculis, fed & evolvendis in æternum.

Vt autem exordiar, hæc de regionū nuperrime detectarum amplitudine habeo, quæ ipfe oculis vidi, quæque Ludovicus Paez de Torres, Architalaffus Majeftati Regiæ nunciavit, longitudo earum, quanta totius eft Europæ, Afiæ minoris ufque ad Mare Cafpium, Perfiæ, cum infulis maris mediterranei, &

Oceani

Exemplar libelli Regi Hisp. oblati.

Oceani omnibus, Anglia ex Scotia comprehensis, cum Hibernia. Incognita hæc terra, est quarta mundi pars, ut bis facile & regna omnia, & regiones, dominia, quibus Rex hodie imperitat, ambitu suo possit complecti. Nō habent hæ regiogiones vicinos Turcas, Mauros aliasve nationes, quibus pro more est, rodere vicinas ditiones: Subjacēt omnes Zonæ torridæ, pars lineæ Æquinoctiali subjacet, latitudinis graduū nonaginta: si vero penitius inspiciātur erūt tales quæ Africæ, Europæ, & maximæ parti Asiæ sint Antipodes, ijsque non cedāt: Notatu dignum, regiones sub quindecim gradibus à nobis perlustratas, Hispaniā nostram fertilitate superare: hinc conijcio, alias altitudini earum oppositas, Paradiso non esse dissimiles.

Scatet totus hic tractus inumerabili incolarum multitudine, alij candidi, alij fuci, alij mulati Hispanicâ linguâ: nonnullis capilli sunt nigri, longi fluentes, quibusdam crispi, villosi, alijs flavi, & rari: ea diversitas magni inter eos commercij, crebrique conventus argumentum est, solique præstantia: maxime laudandum, quod nullis in mutuas cædes machinis bellicis ruant, nec in argenti fodinis operentur tamen nullis artibus videntur imbuti, nec arces habēt nec mœnia. Regem nec legem. Simplices tantum gentes, in factiones divisæ, nec unquam satis concordes. Arma ipsis hæc quotidiana; Arcus, sagittæ at nullo veneno tinctæ, clavæ, fustes, tela missilia & lignea: Pudēda sna velāt; mūditiei sint studiosi, tractabiles grati in benefactores (expertus loquor.) Hinc spes affulget si placide & amice tractentur, futuros placabiles, dociles, quibusque facile satisfiat: quæ tria maximè sunt necessaria in hisce primordijs, ut gentes hæ Zelo quodam ducantur ad sanctos & salutiferos fines. Ædes earum sunt ligneæ, palmarū frondibus tectæ. Fectilibus utuntur instrumenta textoria norunt, & opera reticulata, imo & retibus utuntur: Marmorarij sunt, Tibias, Tympana, cochlearia, omniaque ejus generis è ligno fabricantur.

B   Cœmiteria

Exemplar libelli

Cœmiteria ipſis ſunt, & loca precibus dicata: Horti in arcolas & pulvillos pulchrè diſtincti: Maximo uſui ſunt ipſis cochleæ margaritiferæ, ex quibus cuneos, ſcalpra, ſerras, ligones, aliaque ejus generis inſtrumenta formant, etiam ſpherulas collo appendendas: Habent inſulani naviculas adfabrè elaboratas, & trajectui commodiſſimas; certum argumentum ipſis nationes eſſe vicinis magis excultas: nec vanū indicium quod verres & gallos gallinaceos caſtrent.

Panes ex triplici radicum genere conficiunt, quarum maxima ibi copia, proveniunt enim injuſſæ, eaſque torrent, & coquunt guſtui ſunt pergratæ, ſalubres, multi ſucci, diuturnæ: nōnullæ longitudinem unius ulnæ ſuperant, craſſitudine ſemiulnam. Fructus ejus tractus quamplurimi & optimi: Platani ſunt ſectuplices, Amygdali quadruplices: prægrandes Obi, fructus cotoneis malis noſtratibus magnitudine & ſapore nō diſſimiles: nuces innumeræ: mala medica, & citrea, quibus Barbari non veſcuntur, alijque non minus ſuaves, quam prægrandes fructus: multæ inſuper, nec minus craſſæ arrundines Sacchari: nec poma noſtratia ipſis deſunt, immenſus ipſis est palmarum numerus, ex quibus TVBA extempore depromitur, ipſis loco vini eſt Acoti, Mollis, & Seri, nuclei ei ſunt ſuaviſſimi, ipſos fructus cocos Indi nominant, cum virent ſunt ipſis loco Carduorum, ipſa medulla cremorem lactis pene refert ubi maturuerint, terrâ ac mari ipſis cibus & potus ſunt, vieti oleo ſtillāt, lijchnis apriſſimo, & vulneribus eſt inſtar balſami. Ex corticibus tenenorum fructuum lagenulas conficiunt, ejuſque generis vaſcula omnia, interiores vero cortices, ſtuppæ, vel muſco vice ſunt, navium commiſſuris ferruminandis, fiuntque ex ipſis rudentes, funes nautici minores, reſtes, elijchnia bombardica: ex preſtantiſſimâ frondiu parte vela ſcapharum & lintrium contexuntur, tenuiſſimæ ſtoreæ, tegulæ etiam quibus ædes foris - intuſque miniuntur, prælongis erect iſque arborum ſtipitibus contignatæ: ex ijs etiam

fiunt

fiunt tabulæ, hastæ, aliaque armorum genera, Remi, aliaque
domestica utensilia, idque notatu dignissimum, hæc palmeta
vinearum instar esse, ex quibus toto anno leguntur vina, sine
ullis laboribus ullo sumptuum, temporisve dispendio. Ole-
rum variæ species nobis visæ, Cucurbitæ Bledi magni & parvi,
fabæ omnia legumina. De carnibus hæc habeto, maxima por-
corum ibi copia, Gallinarum, caponum, perdicum, anatum,
turturum, columbarum: palumbes & capræ alteri Capitaneo
visæ: de vaccis quoque & bubalis sermo erat Indis. Piscium
genus varium: ibi Harghi, pescereijes, lizæ, lingulacæ, Salmo-
nes, Meri, Alosæ, Macabises, Casanes, Pampani, sardæ, rajæ,
cuculi, chitevieje, anguillæ, porci marini, chapini, rubiæ, al-
mexæ, gammari, alijque complures, quorum nomina & numerus non occurrunt, maxima enim copiâ iuxta naves a socijs
capti. Quæ si diligenter perpendantur, conjici potest, quanta
deliciarum varietas ex tanta omnium rerū affluentia, hauriri
poterit, ita ut nec condita ulla, imo ne Marci panes desiderari
poterint, rejectis omnibus extraneis: superunt etiam nauticis
usibus necessatia, butyrum; Petasones, acetum, aromata, om-
nisque generis condimenta. Notatu dignum, multa ipsis esse
nostratibus non dissimilia, majori copiâ quam apud nos, ita
ut ea tellus videtur palmā Europæ eripere gignendo, produ-
cendoque omnia: mittit enim argentum & uniones, Capita
neus alter in historia sua aurū sibi visum commemorat. Tres
igitúr producit pretiosissimas rerum species, à natura hominibus concestas. Nō desunt nuces myristicæ, mastiche, zinziber,
piper (testus sum oculatus) norunt Cinnamomum, mirum si
non nascantur cariophylla, cum affluant omnibus aromati-
bus, eoque magis quod hæ terræ parallelæ sunt regionibus
Tarrenatæ atque Bachan: nec deest materia conficiendi seri-
cum, pitam, Saccharum, Anir, Superbiunt Ebeno, alijsque
lignorum generibus ex quibus naves fiant, cum suis velis, ac
triplici ad rudentes materie, quarum una canabi nostræ non

dissimilis

Exemplar libelli
diffimilis: Olem iftud Cocorum fit ex galagala, vicem picis
liquidæ præftans. Vidimus fpeciem quādam refinæ, qua In-
dipiraguas fuasi. lintres picant: Cumque ipfis non defint capræ, & vaccæ, nec carnium, corij, fevi, arvinæ erit penuria. A-
pes nobis vifæ, mellis ac Ceræ argumentum funt, & præter
hæc, multa milia nobis incognita pollicentur. Situi vero regionum fi accedat induftria, cum ibi tanta fit rerum terrâ naf-
centium copia, non exigua noftratium ibi gignendarum eft
fpes (quarum nonnullas fertiliffimas præftantiffimafque in
Peruvia Hifpaniaque nova provenientes, eo decrevi tranfferre)
Hæc ita conjuncta, terram iftam ita ditatura videntur, ut non
tantum indigenis fuftentandis fufficiant, fed & Americam,
Hifpaniamque fuperfluis ditare poterunt, fi modo non defint qui huic operi manus auxiliatrices adhibeāt. Littora enim
tantum à nobis luftrata illuftriffime Rex, indicio nobis funt,
quid ex intimis regionum penetralibus fit fperandum, fpondeo tanta commoda, tantafque divitias, quantas hodie ex noftris Indis haurimus, animus nobis fuit tantum eas detegere,
non penitus perluftrare, nec licuit ob invalitudinem, aliafque
caufas fingula indagare, cum nec unus menfis fufficeret fed
duodecimum totius anni menfes, ut fingula quæ terra certâ
anni tempeftate nafcantur, notarem. Neque Indi iftarum regionum indigenæ, æftimari debent ijfdem cupiditatibus quibus nos duci, fed eos effe, qui hoc unum defiderant ut ætatem
fine ullis laboribus, corporis defatigatione, moleftijs tranfi-
gant, nec ita ut nos vili lucro inhiantes, aut curis torquentes.

Tantas commoditates vitæque fuavitates & delicias eo loci homo percipiet, quantæ ex folo amæniffimo, cultiffimo, tē-
peratiffimo fperari poffint: Solum eft furvum, pingue & fœ-
cundum, atgilla paffim abundans, ftruendis ædificijs idonea, &
lateribus, & tegulis, nec defunt lapides vivi, marmora fi cuj
animus erit fplendide ædificare. Lignis ad opera quæque regio abundat, pulchræ in eâ planities, campi, ut plurimum ri-
vulis,

vulis, foffis, amnibus divifi, præ altæ, & quidē fiffæ rupes, paffim quam plurimi torrentes, fluvij, in quibus commodè extruantur hydromylæ, Azenæ, traphiches, aliæque aquarum moles. Non deerunt Effeni, Salinæ, & quæ fertilitatem foli arguunt, crebra canneta, in quibus cannæ craffitudinem fex palmorum fuperant, & fructus etiā refpondēt, ipfa in fummitate tenues & præduri, cortice levi: etiam filices Madritēfibus non cedētes.

Sinus divorum Philippi & Iacobi littore viginti leucarum expanditur, planè illimis, tutus noctu & interdiu intrātibus, pagis frequēs, quorum fumos luce mediâ, ignes & faces noctu fæpe eminus confpeximus.

Portus cui nomen eft Veræ cruci, ita latè patet, ut mille navium capax, fundus etiam ei illimis, arenâ nigricanti, vacua fyrtibus, imo anchoram figere licet ad altitudinem plus minus quadraginta ulnarum; inter oftia duorū fluminum, quorum alter Bætim magnitudine fuperat, pulvinus eft, quem vulgus barram vocat, ad profunditatem duarum ulnarum, quæ cata fcopia, & pataffas tranfmittit, alterum Scaphæ noftræ tuto navigabant, aquatum euntes, nullo delectu, cum ad ejus ripam aquarum limpidiffimarum maxima fit copia. Littus, quo exonerātur naves, patet trium plus minus leucarum fpatio, nigricantibus, minufculis, & majufculis filicibus munitū, navibus fuburrandis aptiffimis, quod nullus finus apperet, herbifq; frondētibus vireret, duximus Oceano non pulfari, arborefq; omnes quod in fublime exrectæ, nec hâc vel illâ in partē inclinantes, duximus regionē illâ nullis fere tēpeftatibus infeftari.

Nec præteriundū filetio, ifta amænitate, portū infignē & cōmendabilē, ut & Theffala Tēpe fuperet Sole nōdū orto chilias avium variarū harmoniâ fuâ audientiū animos reficiebat, lufciniæ merulæ, coturnices, acāthides, hirundines innumeres, perequiti (unus tantum pfittacus) voces fuas mifcebāt, nec deerat locuftarum & cicadarum garritus Matutinis & vefpertinis horis fuaviffimos odores ex floribus fpirabat terra, nec azahere

quidem,

quidem, aut alvahaca defideratis. Hinc certo conclufimus äe-
rem regionis effe fuaviffimam, ipfamque Naturam omnium
Matrem optimam ibi fervare temperiem: Portus hi & finus
eo etiam nomine commendantur, quod præftantiffimis infulis adjuncti funt, præfertim feptem, de quibus fama, fe por-
rigere, ad deucentas leucas, certo nobis conftat unum quinquaginta leucas complecti ambitu fuo, duodecimum vero
leucis ab ipfo portu abeft. Vt illuftriff. Rex uno verbo omnia
complectar. Hoc in finu & portu fub 15⅔ graduum altitudine
ftatim fplendidiffima, & populofiffima Vrbs ftatui poteft,
omnes etiam incolæ optatiffimis opibus, & commoditatibus
gaudebunt, eafque communicabunt Provincijs Chili, Peru,
Panamæ, Nicaraguæ, Gattimalæ, Novæ Hifpaniæ, Terrenatæ,
& Philippinis, quibus omnibus tu Rex longè latèque impe-
as; quod fi & has quas offero tuo Imperio ampliffimo ad-
junxeris, eas tanti facio, ut (præterquam quod merito principes funt aliarum) multis alijs tam pretiofarum mercium a-
bundantiâ, quam opulentiâ longe palmam eripiant, etiam
Chinæ, Iaponi, imo & reliquis Afiæ Infulis. Ita ut verbis cō-
plecti non liceat, quid fentiam, nec ullis nifi Mathematicis
mea fententia probari poteft, quorum judicio ftabit, has regiones fub ipfum ingreffum alere poffe viginti hominū aut Hif-
panorum millia, imo longè non abeft qum exclamen. Hic ille eft mundus, cui Hifpania centrum, hæc corpus, ille peri-
pheria.

Quid in igitur Rex illuftriffime commoditatem loci, tem-
periemque àeris commendem; cujus eft & hoc clariffimum
indicium quod cum noftri, exteri iftorum locorum; ibi verfa-
rentur, nullus tamen eorum morbo ullo correptus eft, licet af-
fiduo laborent, fudent, madeant, aquam bibant jejuni, aut
edant quæ tellus mittit, nec evitent Lunam, Solem, minimè
locis iftis fervidum, de nocte etiam ftragula admittant.

Cum igitur plerique incolarum obefi, & magnæ ftaturæ

fint, nonnulli etiam longævi, licet humi vivant, eximiæ falu-
britatis fignum, fi enim quid folo ineffet vitij, habitarent in
fummis ædibus, ut fit in Infulis Philippinis, alijsque a me lu-
ftratis regionibus, cumque carnes & pifces nullo fale conditi,
biduum perftent incorrupti, cū iftinc allati fructus, ut apud me
videre eft, e duobus intempeftivè decerptis, maximè funt falu-
bres: cū deniq; nulla loca fterilia, nec cardui, nec arbores fpino-
fæ, nullæ radicibus fupra terrā elatis, nec lacunæ, paludes, nullæ
in montibus nives, aut noxij vermes, nulli in fluminibus Cro-
codili, nullæ tam domibus, quam frugibus noxiæ formicæ, ni-
guæ, erucæ, culices nobis vifi funt; Statuo, & affirmo hoc no-
ftrum propofitum effe laudabile, cum tales fint Regiones, quæ
quamplurimis Indiæ locis palmam præripiant, quæ fint inha-
bitabiles, aut vix ob moleftías habitari aut coli poffint.

Hiftoriā recenfui Illuftriff. Rex, Regionum, fplēdidiffima-
rum, nomine Majeftatis Regiæ detectarum, & in poffeffio-
nē tuam fub Regio vexillo detectarum: hoc pacto: Primum
erecta Crux, templumque exftructum, honori Divæ Virginis
Lauretanæ, celebrabantur viginti Miffæ, concurrebant
omnes ut obtinerent indulgentias, Fefto Pentecoftes con-
ceffas, cum folenni fupplicatione Fefto Sacramenti imo fan-
ctiffimum iftud Sacramentum perambulabat incognitas iftas
terras, in quibus tria ftatui vexilla, geminas columnas præ-
ferentia, cūm infignijs Majeftatis Regiæ, ita ut merito dici
poffit, jam jam confirmatum illud. Plus ultrā: & quatenus
funt continens, ad extrema effe devētum. Hæc & reliqua omnia tanquam à fideliffimo Regiæ Majeftatis cliente gefta eo
fine ut hunc titulum Auftraliæ incognitæ Rex nofter reliquis
adjiciat; nomenque toto orbe per omnium homimum ora
volitet, maximam in gloriam Numinis divini, quod terram
hanc detexit, neque in eam perduxit & nunc me falvum Regiæ Majeftati ftitit, eodem animo & mente, quo antea, in hoc
Opus, quod antea fovi, & nunc dignitatis, pietatifque, ergo
deamo

deamo & depereo.

Nec despero ob eam quæ est Majestatis Regiæ in consilijs capiundis prudentia, in gerundis magnanimitas, in fovendis Christiana pietas, negotium hoc summo Zelo procuratum iri, imo ut de futura terrarum istarum jam detectarum cultura certior esse possim. Nec loci amænitas, aut lucri spes, stimulum nobis addere deberent ne deserta essent, sed ut Deus Pater cæli ac terræ conditor, cum filio suo Iesu Christo, unico Salvatore, & Spiritusancti, ab incolis agnoscatur, colatur, invocetur, Satanâ rejecto, qui ab ipsis adoratur. Tum primum operi tanto benedicet Dominus, tantaque emolumenta in gentem nostram redundabunt, ut merito in nos copiæ cornu effusisse gloriari poterimus: contra vero si Romanæ Ecclesiæ perduelles has nostris laboribus detectas regiones invaserint, ut falsa sua dogmata propagent, nostraque destruant, Eheu, quantus labor, quantæ curæ in nos ingruent, imo quæ felici auspicio a nobis cepta, in pejus omnia vertentur, ipsam australiæ incognitæ possessionem sibi ipsis adscribent, funditusque evertent, quod omen avertat Deus optimus maximus.

Ex his non dubito cum Regiæ Majestati constet, quanta damna hæc sunt paritura, imo immensis auri argentique thesauris non resarcienda fore incommoda, imo satis difficulter tanto malo remedium posse inveniri ubi radices egerit.

Hac unâ & solâ viâ adspirat Rex ad regni cælestis possessionem, impendēdo tanto negotio summulam aliquam argenti Peruviani, hinc æternum nomen, Imperium novi Orbis offertur. Et cum nemo sit, qui pro hoc in Regem collato beneficio petat præmium ullum, Ego is sum, simul etiam supplico, ut felicissimis hisce temporibus, quid certi decernatur paratæ sunt naves præsidiatiæ & Parones, longa via mihi obeunda, multaq; adhuc tanto itineri desunt, imo maxima jactura animarum, rerumque spiritualium hac mora fit.

Christophorus Columbus, cum suspicaretur tantum novum
vum

vum Orbum detegi poffe, non deftitit moleftus effe Regi fuo,
ut poffit demitti in oras exteras, multo minus mihi defiften-
dum, cum fim certus de fitu earum regionum, & fum teftis o-
culatus. Supplex igitur Regē oro, ut ex millibus remedijs, u-
num decernatur, ut voti compos reddar, & bono hoc quod in
manibus eft, frui liceat, nō ero difficilis, quin muneri meo me
non defuturum fpondeo. Regium erit fræna inijcere Satanæ,
eique iugum imponere, qui iam dominatur ijs gentibus, tu
Rex imperium fufcipe, fis ipfis Patronus & falvator. Hoc u-
num peto & rogo.

C

See for the engraving: the Dutch edition, hereafter.

Samoiedarum, trahis a rangiferis protractis insidenti
Nec non Idolorum ab ijsdem cultorum effigies.

Regionum Siberiæ, Samojediæ, Tingoëfiæ &

itinerum è Moſcovia, Orientem & Aquilonem verſus eò ducentium, ut à Moſchis ho-
die frequentantur.

 N Moſcoviâ eſt natio, cui nomen Anicouvij
filij, ruſticâ progenie, genealogiam ducens, à
quodam agricolà Anica: Hic agris abundans
adhabitabat flumini VVitſogdæ influenti fluvium Dunam, ab Oriente, lambēti vero à Sep-
tentrione Oſoylam, & Vſtingam centeſimo
inde miliari prope Fanum Michaelis Archangeli arcem ſic
dictā in mare album ſe exoneranti. Hic Anica locuples, multa prole beatus omnibuſque fortunæ donis fruens, acri quadam libidine captus ſtudebat reſciſcere quas terras & regiones
incolerent illi, qui quotānis ad mercatum veniebāt in Moſco-
viam, pretioſis pellibus, alijſque mercibus linguâ, veſtitu, Religione, moribus plane diſſimiles. Samojedas ſe dicentes va-
rijſque nominibus compellantes. Ferebantur hæ nationes
quotannis flumine ſecundo Oſoylam & Vſtingam verſus ad
fluvium Dunam, merces omnis generis cum Ruſſis & Moſchis permutantes, maxime pelles quas Babylonicas dicimus,
ad emporia deferentes.

Hic ANICA, cupidus ſcire, unde hi venirent & quæ loca
incolerent ſpes enim maximarum divitiarum affulgebat, ex
iſtis pellibus quas quotannis importabant clanculum cum
nonnullis amicitiam contraxit, imo decem aut duodecim ſer-
vulos comitatui eorum in patriam adjunxit, hoc ipſis dans
negotij, ut regiones quas tranſirent curioſè exploraret, maxime de eorum moribus, habitaculis, ratione vitæ, geſtibus ſtu-
dioſe inquirerent, ut redeuntes domum, de ſingulis rationem

exactam

exactam redderent, quod & fecerunt, Anica vero reverfos
omnes familiariter fufcepit, amice tractavit, tantum filentio
ipfis impofito, quæ intellexerat condidit animi fui penetralibus, neque cuiquam verbum fecit, fequenti anno cum exteri
ad mercatum venirent, plures focios itineris ex fuis adjunxit,
imo amicos, & fanguine junctos, ijfque commifit merces nō-
nullas vilioris pretij, ut tintinnabula, crepundia, & quales Germania mittit, etiam hi fingula regionum iftarum diligenter
perfcrutati funt, cumque quamplurima deferta, & flumina
emenfi effent, pervenerent ad flumen Obi, ubi contracta cum
Samojedis amicitiâ, notarunt pelles iftic nullo in pretio ha-
beri, fi vero inde exportuntur, divitias maximas ex ijs congeri
poffe, præterea hanc gentem nullis cingi muris fed gregatim,
& pacifice inter fe vivere, a fenioribus populi eos regi, eos effe
immundos in cibo præparando, & ferarum carnibus victitare,
panis & frugum nullam habere notitiam, folertes effe atque
induftrios, fagittis valere, arcus lento quodam & flexibili ligno fieri, lapidibufque acutis, vel pifcium fpinis præmuniri,
ijfque feras trajicere, quarum maximus ibi numerus: pifcium
fpinas ipfis acus effe, & nervos fila, atque ita confuere pelles
quibus veftiuntur, quarum pilos æftate extrorfum hyeme vero introrfum vertunt: Notarunt infuper eos tegere domos
fuas Alcium, aut fimilium animalium pellibus, quas nullo loco habent. Vt omnia uno verbo complectar, emiffarij hi cu-
riofè fingula obfervarunt, maximaque pellium Babylonica-
rum copiâ onufti ad fuos rediere, ex quibus omnia, quæ tan-
topere auebat fcire Anica, refcivit planè, qui fubfequentibus
annis negotiatus eft cum amicis iftarum regionum, & fœdere
junctis, ut eâ negotiatione Anicovij congefferint maximas divitias, multofque agros undique coemerint, latuit hic dolus
omnes vicinos, ignari unde tantæ opes affluerent, nec defuit
ipfis pietas, ædes enim facras nonnullas condidere in fuis pagis: poftea etiam pulcherrimum templum ftruxere in urbe O-
foylâ,

foylâ, ad fluvium Witfogdam, quam habitabant tum temporis, fundamentum albo topho fubftruƈtum erat, ita ut uno
verbo dicam, nullus erat divitiarum modus, néque menfura:
nihilominus profpera hæc fortuna ipfis fufpeƈta fuit, ne ali-
quando felicitatem tantam negaret, ut fæpe evenit, maximè
cum apud exteros maximâ laborarent invidiâ, cum tamen ipfi
caufam non præberent, infigni quadam providentiâ huic malo remedium adhibuere, ut certi effe poffint de ftatu fuo, didi-
cerant illi ex proverbio ufitato apud Mofchos, cui in aulâ non
funt amici, ne homo quidem cenfendus: fit enim plærumque,
ut qui dotibus aliquibus, aut divitijs affluunt in Mofcoviâ, invidiâ præmantur, aut falfo accufentur apud Principem, nifi
vero fautores habeant, ilico indiƈta caufa ad extrema redigun-
tur aut radicitus evelluntur: Hi Anicouvij cum opibus affluerent, non defuit ipfis in aula fautor, qui fecundus a Rege ha-
bebatur, diƈtus Boris Goddenoof, gener Imperatoris Fedor
Iuanovitz, tum temporis regnantis, hic vero Boris defunƈto
focero, in regno fucceffit ut apparet ex Annalibus Mofcoviæ.

Vifum igitur fuit Anicouvijs, huic Boris omnia aperire, ob-
latis primum ei de more muneribus, hoc unum rogantes ut
eorum diƈtis faciles præberet aures, fe quid habere quod toti
imperio ufui effet, & prodeffet: Boris arreƈtis ftatim auribus fe
facilem præbuit, eique aperuit terrarum Samojedæ & Siberiæ fitum, tum quæ ibi eft vifa, & notata, & quãtæ opes huic
Imperio Mofcouitarum poffent affluere, multo quam antè li-
beralius eos excepit: hæc cum fatis planæ ipfi aperuiffent, nihil
tamen de fua negotiatione, in ijs regionibus, & quam teƈtè
cum incolis egiffent, quantafque divitias brevi convafaffent.
Boris ftatim ardere cupiditate, ac velle ifta inquirere, complex-
us eft illos, non fecus ac ex fe natos, & ad dignitates promovit
imò ampliffimo Imperatoris nomine ipfis conceffo diploma-
te cavit, ut fine contradiƈtione terris & agris perpetuo liberè

fruerentur,

fruerentur, eofque pro libitu in hæredes tranfferent, & quod maximum immunes effent ob omni tributo in perpetuū, fic paulatim crevit eorum fortuna; ut etiam fi forte hyberno tēpore in urba Mofcuâ effent, eos fuâ rehi iuffit, quod maximum eft honoris genus, fi deferatur a Magnatibus qualis hic Boris erat, penes eum enim totius regni Imperium. Vbi vero fingula prependiffet Imperatori rem totam aperuit, cui neq; difplicuit, imo maximo deinceps honore hunc B O R I S affecit, eique totum hoc negotium commifit: Ille non fegnis, Ducum magnanimorum, & tenuioris fortune Nobilium quibus favebat, operâ eft ufus, jubebatque ut eos itineris comites fibi adfcifcerent, quos Anicouvij adjungerent, fplendideque fe veftirent more Legatorum, adjunctis infuper aliquot militibus, muneribufque exigui pretij, quæ gentibus largirentur, quas accederent, ijfque hoc in mandatis dedit, ut omnes Vias publicas, vel Regias, Flumina, Sylvas, & loca fingula notarent, etiam ipfa nomina, ut poft reditum de fingulis rationem poffent reddere nec immemor hujus mandati fuit, ut humaniter gentes iftas tractarent, comiter exciperent, interea tamen de commodiffimo loco defpicerēt, ubi Arx, aut propugnaculum quoddam exftrui poffet, imo fi fieri poffet, ut incolas iftarum regionum in Mofcoviam unà fecum adducerent.

Legati hi, veftibus, armis, pecuniâ, donarijs, omnibufque rebus ad iter neceffarijs inftructi, Mofchuâ difcedunt, VVitfogdam poftea apud Anicouvios devenere, qui jam & focios itineris deftinarāt, una & amicos nonnullos, eorumque liberos. Vbi eo deventum fiut, egerunt, fedulo inquirentes, de optimatibus, quibus maximum honorem exhibuerunt, & munufcula obtulerunt, quæ ipfis videbantur maximi valoris, quæ tantâ gratiā apud exteros peperere, ut Mofchos, occurrētes, plaufibus & clamoribus exciperent, ad pedes eorum fe abijcerent, imo ob cultum tam fplendidum pro dijs eos haberent. Interea datâ occafione, cæpere Mofchi interpretibus ufi Samojedis, aliquot
annis

annis in pagis Mofcoviæ addifcēdæ linguæ gratia verfatis, agere
& loqui magnificè de fuo Imperatore, quē infinitis extolle-
bant laudibus, ut Deum terreftrem eum pænè facerent, mul-
taque obiter adijciebant, quibus cupiditate videndi inflámma-
bantur magis ac magis, avebant enim oculis videre ea quæ in-
tellexerant, oblatâ hac occafione ftuduerunt Mofchi, eorum
votis fatiffacere, addebāt & illud fe obfides relicturos, qui dum
in Mofchoviâ Barbari effent, linguam eorum addifcerent: hoc
pacto multorum hominum animos cis Fluvium Obij fibi de-
vinxerunt, qui fe ultro fceptro Mofchorum fubiecerunt pro-
mittentes fingulis annis, in fingula capita, (ne pueris quidem
arcum tractare difcentibus exceptis) binas Sabellorum pelles,
quæ ipfis nullo loco erant, fed Mofchis maximo, imo inftar ci-
melij, eas promiferunt fe fatiffacturos Tribuno ærario, de-
putato, quod & accidit fatis fideliter. Trajecere de hinc legati
Fluvium Obij, & ducentas fere Leucas trans Fluvium, Ortum
& Aquilonem verfus emenfi funt: obtulere fe paffim variæ
ferarum fpecies, limpidiffimi fontes, ftirpes & arbores rario-
res, fylvæ amæniffimæ, etiam nonnulli Samojedæ, quorum a-
liqui Alcibus vehebantur, aliqui rhedis qui a Cervis, & Canibus velocitate cervos fuperantibus trahebantur: Multi deni-
que occurerunt, vifu & admiratione digna, quæ ordine &
fideliter notarunt. Omnibus hifce tranfactis, nonnullos fuo-
rum ut linguam addifcerent, apud Samojedas reliquerunt, &
voluntarios Samojedarum affumferunt, ducentes in patriam
fuam Mofchoviam, feliciffimè iter abfolverunt, & rationem
de fingulis reddidere huic B O R I S, qui verbo tenus omnia
Imperatori recenfuit, feliciffimumque fucceffium. Admirabantur omnes, adductos ad fe Samojedas, jufferuntque ut ede-
rent dexteritatis in fagittando fpecimina, quæ ita docté ab illis
edita, ut fidem fuperent: nummulum enim ad magnitudinem
noftratis dimidiati ftuferi, arbori adfigebant, è cujus confpectu
fecedebant longè, ut vix dignofci poffet, attamen fingulis icti-
bus

bus fcopum feriebant, quod fpectatoribus miraculo fuit, &
admirationi.

Ita è contrario hi Samojodæ mirabantur cum mores & vi-
tam Mofchorum, tum & urbis Mofcuæ fplendorem, fed non
fine horrore intuebantur ipfum Imperatorem, ita fplendidè
veftitum, fi aut equo veheretur, vel lecticâ, a multis equis tra-
heretur, quamplurimus nobilibus non minus fplendide or-
natis cingeretur fatellitibus quadringētis, armis fuis inftructis
publicè obferveretur, nihilominus fonum campanarum admirabantur, quarum in urbe Mofcua infinitus numerus, etiam
luculentiffimas officinas publicas urbis, imo faftum & fplendorem totius civitatis, ut in Deorum thronos fe fublatos fuf-
picarentur, at hoc unum erat in votis, ut popularibus fuis lice-
ret adeffe, eifque rerum vifarum Hiftoriam narrare, quin bea-
tos fe prædicabant, fi tanto Imperatori fe poffent fubjicere,
quem plane pro Deo quodam habebant. Cibos à Mofchis ap-
pofitos avide comedebant, gratiores enim palato eorum erant
carnibus crudis, quibus in patriâ vefcuntur, aut pifcibus vento
duratis & merito.

Tandem eo devenit, ut Imperatorem in Principem fuum
delegerint, etiam populares longè lateq. diffusos, ad idem fœ-
dus induxerint, eumque fupplices rogarunt, ut dignaretur eos
eo honore, ut Gubernatores nonnullos mitteret, a quibus re-
gerentur, quibufque tributa prædicta perfolverent.

De idololatria iftarū gentium, nulla mentio, fed non fubla-
ta eft, non dubito tamen Chriftianam fidem apud eos facile
poffe propagari, fi modo idonei fatis, & maxime pij verbi divini præcones eô mitterentur, quod opus maximè Chriftianum
non intermittetur, ubi Mars ab ipfis exulaverit.

Hifce omnibus ita tranfactis Anicouvij, ad magnas dignitates afcenderunt, magnaque paffim immunitate quin & Imperio in finitimis terris donati, latifundia centū inter fe miliaribus diffita, ad fluvios Dunam, VVitfogdam, & Soehnam pacificè

cificè poffidentes, ita ut potentiffimi, opulentiffimique fint & habeantur, nullufque fit honorum & dignitatum modus.

Deliberatum imo ftatutum jam apud Mofchos, deligenda ad flumen Oby, & finitimis Regionibus, loca, natura fua munita, ut in ijs ftruant, & præfidiario milite firment Arces, eoque mittant Gubernatorem publicum qui magis ac magis vicinas terras detegat, regnoque adjiciat: Nec defuit eventus primum enim ftructæ funt validæ arces aliquot, ad formam Murorum Gallicorum, trabibus directis perpetuis in longitudinem, fine faxis, paribus intervallis, quæ multo aggere intus effarciuntur ufque ad iuftam altitudinem, quæ poftea præfidio munitæ funt. Tantaque in dies eo mittitur hominum multitudo, ut nonnullis locis jam collectæ fint civitates, è Polonie, Tartaris, Ruffis alijfque nationibus inter fe mixtis. Omnes enim exules, homicidæ, proditores, fures & qui morte digni eô relegantur: quorum nonnulli aliquandiu in vinculis detinentur, aliqui liberè vivunt aliquot annis, refpectu fceleris commiffi, hinc populofæ tandem coalverunt hominum focietates, quæ unâ cum arcibus integrum conficiunt regnum, confluentibus eo quotidie multis tenuioris fortunæ hominibus, ut fruantur immunitatibus, ibi conceffis.

Ifti tractui nomen eft SIBERIA, urbi in eo exftructæ SIBER, fub initium facinorofi, ubi inaudiffent nomen SIBERIÆ, non aliter expavefcebant, quam flagitiofi apud Amfterodamenfes famofum illud PISTRINVM, ablegabantur enim ftatim Siberiam verfus, jam vero pœnæ iftius frequentia, abijt in contemtum, Optimatis adhuc, & nobiles Mofchi fiquando incurrerunt in Principis indignationem, Siberiæ nomen abominantur, cum fæpe eô ablegentur, cum totâ familiâ, ubi Magiftratui fubjiciuntur dum Imperatoris ira fedetur, & in patriam revocantur.

D

Itinerum ducentium, & fluviorū labentium

è Moſcoviâ Orientem & Aquilonem verſus, in Siberiam, Samojediam & Tingoëſiam, ut a
Moſchis hodie frequentantur.

Item,

Nomenclaturæ oppidorum in Siberia a Moſ-

chis conditorum, quæ prorex gubernat, etiam incognita explorat, & occupat, ita ut in magnam
Tartariam fere penetrarit.

 X urbe Soil, ad fluvium VVitſogdam, quem
accolunt Anicovij, contendunt adverſo flu-
mine, donec perveniant Iavimiſcum, oppidulum iſtud a Moſchis conditum, & Soilâ
ſeptendecim dierum, itinere fere diſſitum,
multis fluminibus & ſylvis moleſtum. Naſ-
citur hic VVitſogda, ex montibus Ioëgorijs, Tartariæ ad Auſtrum conterminis, Boream verſus ad ipſum Oceanum uſque
extendentibus: ex ijſdem labitur & Petziora, qui cis fretum
VVaygats Oceano ſe immiſcet. Iaviniſco digreſſi, trium hebdomadarum itinere emenſo, Neemū flumē attingunt, quod
leni per ſylvas fluit agmine, unde & nomen habet Ne-em,
quod latinis mutum, illud navigant pæne quinque dies, hinc
merces ſuas ad leucam unam tranſſerunt ad VViſſeram flumen, quod è rupibus Ioëgoriorum montium appendicibus
profluit, quas Moſchi Camenas vocāt: tum feruntur novem
dies continuos ſecundo hoc flumine donec perveniant Zoil
Camſcoy, a Moſchis conditum, & refocillandis mercatoribus
dicatum, terreſtri itinere profecturis, hic VViſſera fluvius,
continuato curſu ſuo, tandem CAMO ſe miſcet, Viatram
Moſcoviæ oppidum lambens, maximo flumini Rha, quod &

volga

Volga dicitur illabitur, quod fe feptuaginta oftijs exonerat in mare Cafpium, ut ex fide dignis accepi, teftibus oculatis.

Cum aliquandiu moras traxiffent in urbe Soil Camfcoy, multos equos eduxere eò loci, imo hoc tempore habitatur à Ruffis & Tartaris, pagis, & pecoribus affluentibus. Mercatores itaq; paululum expeditiores ad iter, equis merces fuas imponentes, per montes iter faciunt, abjetibus, pinis, & raris arboribus luxuriantes, inter hos montes traijciunt flumen Soibam, hinc Cofnam, utrumque Septemtrionem verfus labitur. Hi mōtes in tres partes distribuuntur, quarum duæ priores, biduij, tertia, quatridui itinere fuperantur. Ac primæ nomen eft Coofvinfcoij Camen, alteri Cirginfcoj Camen, tertiæ, Poduinfcoij Camen. Hi montes longè diverfi funt ab ijs, quos fuperarunt paulo ante, fylvæ multo pulchriores funt, & denfiores, varias etiam paffim ftirpes producentes. Hæc deferta etiam a Tartaris & Samojedis frequentantur, ut tantum pelles pretiofas hifce in locis venentur Imperatori Mofchorum. Montes Podvinfcoij Camen, reliquis altitudine fuperant, nubibus paffim & nivibus tecti, ideoque viatoribus fatis molefti, fed paulatim declives fiunt. Hinc Vergateriam appropinquāt, ubi fubfiftendū, dum ver appetit, caufa eft fluvius Toera, qui vadofus id tēporis, & proximis iftis locis nafcatur. At vere novo, gelidus canis cum mōtibus humor liquitur, & magnis accrefcunt auctibus amnes, fcaphis & lēbis traijcitur.

Vrbs hæc Vergateria, primum terræ Siberiæ eft oppidum, ante annos viginti & unum conditum, & nonnullis alijs in ijfdem regionibus: civibus abundat, a quibus agri vicini, ut in Mofcovia fit, coluntur. Hic refidet Prorex, ut ita dicam, aut Gubernator, qui maximam quotannis, initio veris, frugum, annonæque copiam, omnibus præfidiariò milite munitis Siberiæ arcibus, diftribuit, imo & Mofchis trans flumē Obi degentibus hoc pacto profpicit cum ibi non colatur tellus, & Samojedæ, ferinâ victitent: Secundó Toerâ flumine navigantes quinquiduum, Iapanfin deveniunt, oppidulum ante

biennium

biennium ftructum, & colonis infeffum, hinc rurfus Toera
feruntur, fic biduum progreffi, cogūtur obviæ compendium
anfractuofofque ejus meatus, fæpe fe terræ committere, hæc
vero loca jam paffim habitant Tartari & Samojedæ, pecuarij
plærique omnes & navicularij.

Tandem emenfo Toerâ, ad ingens flumen Tobol deveniunt, ducentas fere leucas à Vergateria diftans, & hinc Tinnam
navigant, oppidum populofum, à prædictis coditum: quamplurimi etiā rhedis, hiberno tēpore, duodecim dierum itinere Iapanfi Tinnam perveniunt, atque hic maxima pellium
pretiofarum, inter Mofchos Tartaros, Samojedafque vigent
commercia; oportuna hæc navigatio ijs, qui tantum uno
femeftri abeffe volunt domo, quamplurimi tamen ulterius
penetrant, imo ipfum flumen Obij tranfeunt, regiones Oriē-
tales, & Meridionales perambulātes.

Tinnâ Tobofcam, Siberienfium oppidorum Metropolim
devenitur, ubi fupremi Proregis Siberiæ ac Mofchorum fe-
des eft, & quotannis huc omnium vicinarum Vrbium tributa
deferuntur, tā cis quā citra collecta, & publico cōmeatu munita, in Mofcoviā ad Imperatorē deducūtur: & hic fummo jure
jus dicitur, a Prorege cui tanta potentia, quāta in ipfa Mofcoviâ, eiĝ; quotquot in Samoiediâ, Siberiaĝ; gubernatores fafces
deferunt. Vigēt proterea hic rerum e Mofcoviâ deportatarum
cōmercia, confluētibus eò ex tractū Auftrali, & ab ultimâ fere
Tartariâ Tartaris, aliarumq; gētiū hominibus, ita ut quo magis, divulgatur regionū iftarū fama, eò frequētiores cōcurrāt.
Vnde Mofchis non exigua proficifcitur utilitas, qui tā pacificè
has gētes fubjugarūt, eifĝ; ita addictæ, ut de earu fide defperā-
dū minime fit. Paffim etiā ftructa ab ijs tēpla, in quib₃ Græca
exercetur religio, quæ Ruffis quāplurimifĝ; Septemtrionali-
bus facrofancta eft, licet non paucis fuperftitionibus deprava-
ta; Talis autē eft ftatus, nemo invitus relligionē hāc vel illam
amplecti cogitur, fed à Ruffis media quædam nō violenta ad-
hibētur, quibus homines iftos lucri faciāt, ducāt, & nō cogāt.

Sita

Sita eft urbs Tobolfca, ad fluvium Iirtim, qui rapidiffimo flumine, inftar Danubij a parte meridionali ortum ducens in Oby fe exonerat, qui & ex eodem tractu videtur labi, alteram urbis partem lambit fluvius Tobol, unde urbi nomē eft: cui fe mifcet fluvius Taffa, ab aquilone ex montibus maritimis ortum ducens, ad hujus ripam Mofchi nuper urbem cōdidere, quam Poliem dixere, colonijs è Siberia ductis, auxere, hac folā de caufā, quod ager fertiliffimus eam cingat, nec defint Sylvæ amæniffimæ, nutricolæ variarum ferarum, pantherarum, lyncium, vulpium, fabellorum & martarum. Diftat vero Polienum Tobolfcā duarum hebdomodarum itinere in Aquilonem. Iirtis fluvius pari ferè a Tobolfcā fpatio, fe commifcet fluvio Oby, ad cujus oftium oppidum Olfcoygorotum conditum fuit, at poftea juffu gubernatoris Siberiæ dirutum, caufa vero prodita non fuit, eam tamen hanc fuiffe fufpicor, intenfum frigus, vel quod mari vicinius effet, damnum aliquod, aut inundationem metuebant, imo maximum periculum fi forte populis quamplurimis ditatum effet. Cumque fluvius Obi maximarum aquarum copiā redundet, & ingentem vicinarum terrarum partem tanquam brachio amplectatur, & circumfluat, atque ita in fe refluat, eamque magnam infulam faciat, in eā novam urbem, quinquaginta miliaribus à mari diffitam condidere, quam Zorgoet nominant.

Hinc adverfo flumine navigantes, raro utuntur velis, vel quod languidum fpirēt venti, vel montes obfint, licet ubique fere luxuriet Oby, fcaphas tamen funibus protrahant, planè eo modo quo Mofcoviæ fluvios fuperant.

Ducentis fupra Zorgoet leucis emenfis Narmifcoy arcem tredecim adhinc annis exftructam deveniunt, cum fummus Siberiæ Gubernator nonnullos emiferat, terras humano generi commodas, atque urbibus condendis idoneas indagaturos, eamque id temporis ftruxere, atque armato milite munivere, tractu per quam amæno, falubri, tepido, fertili, & in quo

ferarum

ferarum & avium chiliades, hinc tandem incolis ditata, excre-
vit in civitatem, cumque fita fit in Euronotum, ijs id negotij
datum eft, ut ad ulteriora, calidioraque loca pedetentim afcen-
derent, & fincerè ubique negotiarētur obvias quafque gentes
humaniter tractarent, quo latius tandem regnarent, & Ruffi-
cum imperium extenderetur; cumque gregatim fæpe terras
interiores exploraffent ultra cētum leucas, amæniffimos quidem, fed cultoribus vacuos invenire tractus, fed abhinc annis
decem, cum adverfo flumine Oby, ducēta milaria fuperaffent,
in regionem non minus uberem, quam amœnam inciderunt,
moderatè calidam, nullo pænè incommodo laborantem, frigoribus omnibus liberam; hinc occafio oblata redeundi in
Siberiam, atque Imperatori Mofcoviæ fignificandi. ubi id
temporis imperabat B O R I S G O D D E N O O F, cui hoc
curæ erant, ilico in mandatis dedit Gubernatori Siberiæ, ut
colonias eo mitteret, urbemque conderet; nec caruit fucceffi-
bus, Arcem ftatim condidit, loci oportunitate, & formâ fuper-
bam, adjunctis nonnullis caftellis, ut nunc nomen urbis audi-
at Toom, quod intellexerint Tartarorum multitudinem eò
loci olim confediffe, à quibus hæc urbs ob eximiam fitus a-
mœnitatem nomē hoc accepit, quorum Rex erat Altyn, hinc
multarum gentium locis campeftribus fe detinentium hæc
Vrbs impetus fæpe fuftinet, nunc vero cum viribus & armis
valeat, in Regnum novum furget. Cæterum intra urbem
Toom, & arcem Narmifcoy, & Sibiriam, quamplurimæ dete-
guntur gentes, quæ fe Oftacki nominant, & cum Tartaris, Samojedis, & Ruffis in unum jam corpus coäluere, amicè inter
fe negotiantes, auro varijfque mercium generibus. Quamplurimi ipfis Reges imperitant, quales in India, non longè la-
teque dominantes: & uno verbo dicam, Mofchi in illo tractu
incredibiles fecere progreffus & ulteriores fperamus. Intra
Oby & Iyrtim Fluvios quamplurimæ arces, urbefque condi-
tæ funt, eò fere tempore cum Tobolfcam conderent, opibus

jam affluentes, quaram incolæ funt Mofchi Tartari Samojedæ, omnes manfueti; earumque prima eft Tara hinc Obi &
Iirtis. Itinere decem dierum diftant, etiam illa quam Iorgoet
dicunt, condita ante quindecim annos, etiam Befou, & Man-
ganfeifcoygorad, fitæ ad Auftrum, at in parte occidentali fluminis Obi, incolæ ftudent ulterius progredi. Cis Obi fitæ
funt urbes Tobolfca, Siberia, Berefou, & quamplurimæ aliæ,
ad diverfa flumina, in dies exftruuntur. Trans Obi funt Narim, & Toomen, ijs in locis incolæ utuntur cervis, loco equorum etiam canibus velocibus, quos pleriq; pifcibus vento duratis educunt & nutriunt, quò fint validiores.

Iorgoet in Infula quadam fluminis Obi fita eft.

Ab urbe Narim orientem verfus iter facientibus occurrit
fluvius T E L T A, in cujus ripa arx Congofffcoi condita eft,
etiam præfidio munita, hujus incolis cum Narimenfibus à
Gubernatore Siberiæ ante feptennium in mandatis datum ut
ulterius in Orientem pergerent, & quæ incognitæ gentes iftic
viverent indagarēt cumq; decem hebdomadarum iter emenfi effent, per deferta ampla, loca amæna, arboribus & fluminibus varijs ornata, deprehenderunt magalia quædā in campis,
& infignē hominū multitudinē, fed cum ductoribus Samoie-
dis ac Tartaris uterētur, locorum iftorum gnaris, nihil timue-
runt. Appropinquātes vero reverēter, & officiofè exceperunt,
& per interpretes Tingoëfi fe vocari dixerunt, & ripā fluminis Ienefeia accolere, quā àb Euronoto fluere affirmabāt, fed
de origine eius nihil conftabat, & latitudine fuperabat flumē
Obi. Accolæ hi ftrumis à mento propendentibus erant defor-
mes, & glocientes inter loquendum ut Pavones Indici, lingua
eorum non diffimilis a Samoiedarum, cum fe mutuo in multis intelligerent.

Fluvius Ienefeia, magnitudine Obi fuperans, ab Ortu ex-
celfis montibus veftitur, ignivomis nonnullis, & fulphureïs,
ob occafu, planus eft, eximè fertilis, herbis, arboribus, floribus

bus virēs, & fructibus abundās nec deeſt aviū omniū varietas. Notatu dignum flumen hoc verno tempore campos ſpatio ſeptuaginta leucarum inundare, non ſecus ac de Nilo Ægypti narrant Hiſtoriæ, non minus edocti Tingoeſi, trans ipſum flumen, & in vicinis montibus degunt, donec refluat, relapſo flumine ad campos redeunt, armentaque ſua ad pabula conſueta, & planitiem reducunt.

Tingoëſi humanitatis veſtigia præſeferunt, inducti ab hortationibus Samojedarum, eidem Gubernatori ſe ſubjecerunt, quem loco Dei honorabant. Non licuit cognoſcere quod numen illi colerent hactenus, credo evenire negligentia Moſchorum, non ſedulo ſingula inquirentium.

Non profecto admirandum, fretum hoc Waygats, quotannis glacie obſtrui, a parte boreali, cum magna iſta fluminæ Obi & Ieneſeja, aliaque compluræ vicina nobis adhuc incognita, tantos glaciei acervos, tantæque craſſitudinis montes evomant, ut fidem ſuperent, fit enim nonnumquam veris initio, ut glacies præ craſſitudine & multitudine ſua, in maritimis locis, totas a terris abrūpat ſylvas, hinc eſt quod ad littora freti Waygats tanta paſſim conſpiciatur lignorum undique confluentium copia, cumque in illo ad Novam Zemlam freto intenſiſſimum ſit frigus, nihil mirum, ſi in ipſâ freti anguſtiâ tam immanes coacerrentur, & concreſcant glaciei moles, ut in ſexaginta aut minimum quinquaginta ulnarum craſſetudinem coaleſcant, ut dimenſi ſunt illi, qui ab Iſaaco le Maire navigiolo quodam eo miſſi ierant.

Sed ad rem. Suſcepere Moſchi poſtea iter paulo ulterius, ſuperantes Ieneſejam, ſed rectâ in Orientem, non deflectentes Auſtrum verſus, comitibus Tingoëſijs, ex quibus didicerât complures gentes incognitas, habitare Auſtralem partem, & Reges eorum perpetua inter ſe bella gerere; ſed cum aliquot dies iter feciſſent ſine fructu, ad ſuos rediere. Tingoëſijs tamen in mandatis dedere, ut penitius illos tractus luſtrarent

E

amicitiam

amicitiam omnem pollicerentur quod & factum, faedus
enim cū illis pepegere, difcedentes ex oris iftis, Mofchos, faede-
ratos Samojedas, ac Tartaros ipfis reliquerūt, muneribus non
neglectis. Sequenti anno Tingoëfij emifere nonnullos e
fuis, rectâ in Orientem, ulterius aliquanto quam antea progreffi, inciderunt tandem in quendam alium fluviū, Ienefeiâ
quidem minorem, velocitate non difparem, cujus curfum aliquot dies fubfequentes, deprehenderunt homines quofdam,
quos curfu antevertētes apprehenderunt, fed linguâ diffimiles
erant, fed certis quibufdam jndicijs & vocibus Barbarorum,
Om Om fubinde ingeminantium, cōjecerunt ab altera fluvij
parte crebra audire tonitrua; & ftrepitus hominum, ipfum vero flumen digito monftrātes, Peifida dicebant, hinc Tingoëfij, & Tartari colligebant id nomen fluvij effe: at poftea co-
gnorunt Mofchi, fonitus campanarum Om Om fignificari,
repetentes vero patriam, nonnullos accolarum fluvij fecum
duxere, fed in itinere omnes perierunt, an metu, an aeris info-
lentiâ incertum eft, dolebant profecto, omnes comites, tam
Tingoefij, quā Samojedae eorum interitum, redeuntes enim
afferebāt effe homines ingeniofos, formâ honeftâ, oculis par-
vis, facie planâ, colere fufco, & ad luteum vergente.

Hoc cum cognoviffent Mofchi ex Samojedis, a regionibus Tingoëfiorum in Siberiam redeuntibus, ftatim cupiditate
inflammati fuere, ulteriora inveftigandi petētes a Prorege itineris comites, qui ftatim petitioni annuit, cōceffâ fimul magnâ militum manu, eâ lege ut fingula difpicerent, Tingoëfios,
Samojedas, ac Tartaros conjungerent, quod & factitatum, fep-
tingenti enim viri bellicofi, trajecerunt Fluvium Oby, & Samojedarum ac Tingoëfiorum terris trajectis devenerunt ad
Ienefejam flumen, quo trajecto ad ulteriora perrexerunt, du-
cibus Tingoëfijs, qui non tantum anteambulonum obibant
munus, fed & de cōmeatu omnibus profpiciebant, captis mirâ
quedā dexteritate avibus, Cervis, capris, alijfque varij generis
feris,

feris, nec pifcium è fluvijs paffim deerat copia, tandem ad Pefidam flumen perventum, ad cujas ripam tentoria fixere, donec fieret navigabile, proximo Vere, quod inftabat, cum vero folveretur trajicere illud non aufi fuere, fonitu ifto, de quo antea inaudierant, fatis clarè percepto, quem certo judicabant, effe campanarum, flante vero ab ulteroire Pefidæ ripa vento, percipiebant ftrepitum equorum & hominum, nonnumquam vela ipfis vifa, at perpauca, quæ fecundo flumine navigabant, at quadrata, qualia hodie Indorum: at eo loci ubi primum conftiterant nullos homines deprehenderunt, etiam moram trahentes eâ in regione, notarunt flumen Vere novo augeri, periculum tamē ex eo nullum, cum ripa utrimque fit præalta. Sub Autumnum revertentes, narrarunt quantopere delectati fuerint loci amœnitate. Menfibus Aprili & Majo præcipuè, quanta iftic ftirpium, rariorum florum, fructuum, arborum, avium, ferarum, armentorum copia, at Mofchi fuavitatibus hifce non capiuntur, nil nifi lucrum vile meditantes, in cæteris planè faxei funt. De veritate vero non dubitandum cum iuramento omnia & fingula confirmarint.

Hæc fama cum in Aula Mofchorum percrebuiffet, Borius Imperator, reliquique regni Proceres admirabantur quam maximè, imo illos invafit cupido fingula diligenter perfcrutandi; Ideoque ftatutum erat, annuente ipfo Imperatore èo mittere Legatos, muneribus Regijs inftructos, comitibus Tartaris, Samojedis, & Tingoefijs, ut ripam ulteriorem fluminis Peifidæ luftrarent, ejufque fitum notarent, etiam amicitiam cum Regibus, populifque contraherent, fi qui effent, aut regerent, fingula obfervarent, reverfi diftinctè narrarent, maximè quæ antea de Campanarum fonitu allata, fed caruerunt hæc omnia eventu, ob bella civilia nuperrimè inter Mofchos exorta, ut ex eorum defcriptionibus fufius liquebit, quas brevi Deo volente publicas faciemus.

Interea

Interea tamen Gubernatores non defuerunt fuo muneri, non ceffantibus hifce bellis in eos tractus emifere nonnullos, multis e Siberiâ civibus voluntarijs comitibus, qui cum Tingoëfios tranfiviffent, fluvium Ienefeiam tranfiviffent, pedes reliquū iter abfolverunt, plæriq; tamē vitæ cōmodiori affueti, itineris moleftiâ in viâ ipfâ perierunt, fuperftites vera ea fuiffe deprehenderunt, quæ ab alijs narrata, maximè que dé fonitu Campanarum, & ftrepitu Equorum, hominumq; allata fuerant, at diffuadentibus accolis non aufi fuere flumen traijcere, fed aliquandiu in montibus hæferunt, unde & emicare crebras viderunt flammas, Sulphur, & Lydium lapidem reportarunt, ut de fodinis pretiofis certa fit fides.

Iubebat id temporis Gubernator Siberiæ fcaphas aliquot tegumentis cooperiri, primoq; vere ad fluminis Obi oftium decurrere, & littus legere, donec ad fluvium Ienefejam pervenirent, quæ fe etiam exonerabat in mare, eam adverfo flumine navigarent aliquot dies, Simul etiam eò mittebat nonnullos qui pedeftri itinere ad ripam fluminis contenderent, fcaphas ibi præftolarentur, fi nō incideret in eas, anno elapfo reverterentur. Præcipuè illis qui oras maritimas legeret mādabat, ut fingula notarent, & luftrarent. Præfectum etiā quendā illis adjunxit nomine Lucam, cui maximè negotium omne commifit, dimiffi mari fe commiferunt, atque oftium fluminis Ienefejæ fubiere incideruntque in illos qui pedeftre illud iter fufceperāt qui nōnullos ex comitibus fecūdo flumine fcaphis, ratibusq; ad oftiū Ienefejæ demiferāt reipfâ illi experti funt ita fe rē habere ut conjecerat Gubernator. Interea Luca moritur, cū nōnullis Præfectis cōfultius judicarūt ut quifq; in patriam fuam eâ viâ qua venerat, rediret, quod & feliciter accidit, in Siberiam reduces Gubernatori narrârunt totius itineris fucceffum, de quo ftatim Imperatorem certiorē fecit, tota vero Hiftoria adfervatur in thefaurario público Mofcoviæ, eamque examini fubijcient, cum bella hæc civilia compofita

fuerint,

fuerint, fed defperamus, dolendum profecto fi ita negligantur, tam fertiles infulæ, flumina ampla, Regiones avibus & feris luxuriantes, & ultra ipfum flumen Ienefejam, longè latéque.

Vivebat tum temporis in Mofcovia, amici mei frater, qui his detectionibus comes fuerat, is tabulam quandam, ex fratris jam defuncti ore exceptam, & a fe delineatam nobis tradidit, ipfe vero fretum VVaygats penetraverat, omniumque locorum ufque ad Obi gnarus eft, quis vero fitus regionum ultrâ flumen, cognivit ex alijs; eft fola hæc quam damus tabella rudis duntaxat illius oræ delineatio maritimæ, eamque magnâ moleftiâ mihi comparari, fi vero refcifcerent illi quorum intereft, actum effet de Mofchi illius vita, nomen ideo illius non prodimus.

Fluvius Toas fe exonerat in flumen Obi, profluens ut videtur ex locis Ienefeiæ vicinis, fylvâque vaftâ, ex qua & alius quidam fluvius profluit, proximus Toæ, in Ienefeiâ aquas fuas evomês, adeo ut ab Obi maritimo itinere, per regionem Samoiedarum, duabus tantum terreftri itinere leucis fuperatis, incidant in flumen Torgaef, tandem fecundo flumine in Ienefeiam deveniunt, eft profecto commoda hac via, & a Samojedis & Tingoëfijs non ita pridem inventa.

Hæc funt quæ maximo ftudio refcifcere potui, in Vrbe ipfâ Mofcuâ, de colonijs ductis in maximam Regionem Siberiæ, cum adjacentibus Tartaris Scythicifque nationibus: plura nō licuit inquirere, imo difficile fuit, hæc quæ retuli impetrare ab alijs, cum Ruffis maximè difpliceat, fi exteris fecreta regni innotefcant.

Ifaac Maffa Haerlem.

N præfatione poſtremæ editionis hujus libelli, cum agerem de deſcriptione Siberiæ, mentionem feci navigationum à Batavis præſtitarum, ſuper deteĉtione tranſitus, in Chinam, ſupra Novam Zemlam, quas jam enarrare operæ pretium non duxi, cum ſatis ab alijs deſcriptæ, & in theatrum publicum ſint productæ.

Sed poſtremâ navigatione eo etiam fine ſuſceptâ, juſſu Illuſtriſſ. D. D. Ordinum, videbar in prologomenis tum temporis, quid majoris momenti promittere, cum alter Præfeĉtus Ioannes Cornelij Anthropophagus, qui anno ſexcenteſimo undecimo á D. D. Ordinibus emiſſus erat, nondum ſecundum iter abſolviſſet, quo ſtudebat Novam Zemlam ſuperare, & in Chinam tranſire. Priori enim itinere, cum ſub Veris initium ſub altitudine ſeptuaginta duorum graduum, triginta minutarum, aſcenderunt poſteà ad altitudinem ſeptuaginta ſex graduum, uſque ad Crucis Inſulam, ad Berefort, hinc, quia glacies ulterius navigandi iter præcluſerat, navemque læſerat, deflexerunt in Lappiam, ad Inſulam Kilduyn, ubi navem cō-ſolidarunt. Interea Dominis Præfeĉtis rerum nauticarum nunciarunt de ſucceſſu, etiam licet via in Chinam non pateret, non ſine commodo ſe redituros, quare hinc ſolventes in Novam Franciam navigarunt, Occidentē verſus deflectentes, ad altitudinē quadraginta ſeptē graduum, diſtātes ſeptuaginta quinq; miliaribus ad Auſtrali promotorio Inſulæ Ba calaos, Inſulā a Canibus diĉtam appulerunt, eadem illa videtur quæ in tabulis noſtris I. des loups marins. Ab hac inſulâ Occidentem verſus littus legere, omnes etiam ſinus, & Inſulas occurrentes, luſtravere, uſque ad altitudinem quadraginta triū graduum, quindecim minutarum, ſuperantes ſexaginta leucas Germanicas, ubi promontorium arenoſum deprehenderunt, quod C. de Sable dixere, nonnumquam in portubus nōnullis

myriades

myriades Incolarum apparuere, qui verecundiæ omnis prodigi, nudi incedunt, dorfum tantum pelle feræ tegentes, ut frigus arceant, quod tum temporis intenfius erat, quā æftate in Novâ Zemlâ: Ifti Barbari, horrebant frigore, dentibus crepitantes, mucum è naribus defluentem, & in pectus apertum dependentem non abftergebant, minus munditiei ftudiofi, non tamen plane erant irrationales, cum ufus Tabaci ipfis fit frequens in Medicinâ, vifuntur enim hic fiftulæ, quibus Tabaci fumos infpirant, unius ulnæ, aut cubitus magnitudine, artificiofe fculptæ, imagine ad ipfum orificium, Divi cujufdam meo judicio, fedentis flexis genibus, clunibus in calcaneum demiffis, ut apud eos moris eft, arcubus & fagittis femper incedunt armati, tam fæminæ, quam viri, ut fe ab hoftibus defendant, quod experti funt noftri cum fe cum Præfecto fuo terræ committerent, cum antea in aulâ nauticâ fatis tuto delitefcerent, rogabant enim eos, num is, digito Præfectum monftrantes, dux effet, hoc fuo idiomate, Eft cetcij Capiteyne d'Hollande, refpōdebant noftri, eum effe; Ecce fæmina quædam retrocedens nonnihil à cœtu, fagitta Præfectum jaculata eft, ex quo ictu etiam ilico perijt, nihil minus à reliquis tentatum, ita ut fex cum fuo Præfecto perierint; Sufpicor nonnullos Nationis noftræ homines incolas in oris maritimis Frāciæ novæ, infigni quadā injuriâ affeciffe, hinc in vindictâ erupere fatisiniq;.

A Promontorio de Sable, occidentem verfus navigarunt triginta octo, aut quadraginta miliaria, relinquentes a dextris magnum finum, eumque non luftrarunt: Eò deflectit ora maritima Auftrum verfus, & Euronotum, ad altitudinē unius gradus & quadraginta, triginta minutarum, ubi fe vites vidiffe afferunt craffitudine corporis humani. Sub altitudine vero, quadraginta gr. & 35 mi. finus eft a parte boreali, occidentaliq; tutus, quem noftro idiomate Fuyck dixere, hinc ora maritima occidentem verfus vergit, multis fluminibus luxurianſ, quam longè ante reliquerat altera Navis, ut fecūdum iter

supra

fupra Novam Zemlam tentaret, etiam & hæc paulo poſt domum reverſa eſt, omniaque hæc de Canada, oriſque incognitis rettulere ſocij. Interea illa duĉtu Ioannis Cornelij Anthropophagi, uſque ad glaciem educitur elabitur æſtas, nihil fit, hoc tantum Geographia dignū notarunt, Inſulas Matſijn, & S$_r$. Hugo VVilloughbes non reperiri, & mare eſſe vaſtum, inſulis viduum, intra Novam Zemlam, & Vrſorum inſulam; Digniſſimam vero omnium portuum Novæ Franciæ delineationem nobis communicarunt, ijſque pro hocmunere habenda eſt gratia. Se ſub Climate frigido navigaſſe, teſtimonij loco attulere, fragmētū glaciei, maximæ craſſitudinis, quod adhuc in Autumno, in Aulâ Præfeĉtorum rerum navalium videre erat, dētes etiam Morſarum, & exuvias Vrſæ: nonnulla etiam ex Novâ Franciâ, ſed nullius fere pretij omnia.

Ita animoſæ huic expeditioni (ſi Dis placet) eventus laudabilis defuit cujus autor fuerat Præfeĉtus ille Amerſſortus, qui jaculo imbelli (heu) miſer in Novâ Frâciâ perijt. Perſuadebat ſibi quæ à Guilielmo Barnartio, & Iohāne Hugen, in partibus Borealib⁹ præſtita nō ſatis viriliter geſta eſſe: Addebat & hoc abſurdū, Solē cōtinuo ſuo ſplendore, & calore diebus æſtivalibus, magis ſalē produĉturū, quā glaciē, ejuſdē opinionis cum Heliſæo Roſlijn, Doĉtore Hanovieſi, qui in calce libelli D. D. Ordinibus dicati, aſſerit, viā in Septētrionē juxta oras Tartariæ, in Chinā & Iapā, quò magis ad Polum vergit, eò eſſe calidiorē æſtate; quæ opinio tā rationi, quā experientiæ adverſatur, Sol enim radijs obliquis nihil incēdet, ſed direĉtis; Sed ne ſentētiæ rationi cōſentaneæ, pugnēt cum erroneis experiētiā certā eſſe judicabimus, quæ docet, quo propius ad Polū acceſſeris, eò frigus eſſe intētius, tā hyeme, quā æſtate. Licet omne navigationes, & hiſtoriæ teſtētur, de caloribus ſub lineâ Æqui. & frigoribus intenſiſſiimis, ſub Vrſâ, nō tamē ipſis ſatiſſiat, ad abſurdū rediget eos deſcriptio noſtra Nieulandiæ, intra Groenlandiā, & Novā Zemlam, ſub altitudine ſeptuaginta oĉto, aut oĉtoginta graduum ab Æquatore, quæ mentionem faciet frigoris, non caloris, quem tamen D. Roſlin cum ſocijs aſtruit.

De

De detectione Terræ polaris, fub latitudine
octoginta graduum.

Anno millefimo nonagefimo fexto (cum Illuftrffimi Domini Ordines, bis nonnullos emiferant, ut viam vel tranfitum in Chinam in parte boreali inveftigarent) Confules & Senatores Amfterodamenfes duas emifere naves, quibus præfecti Guilielmus Barentzon Amfterodamenfis, & Ioannes Cornelij Rijp, Enchufanus, hi cum perveniffent, ad altitudinem Promontorij borealis in Norvvegiâ, Occidentem verfus curfum inftituerunt, inducti a Ioanne Cornelij, metuens fi in Orientem deflecteret, ad anguftias freti VVaygats deduceretur, Ideo inciderunt in Infulam quandā, fub altitudine feptuaginta quatuor graduum, triginta minutarum, quā Urforum dixere, ob copiam, unum interfecere, hunc excoriantes, pellē longitudine duodecim pedum fuiffe deprehenderunt : deflectentes hinc Septemtrionem verfus, quinto Iunij, fragmenta glaciei occurrere, quæ fuperarunt, ufque ad decimum nonum ejufdem menfis, tum terram deprehenderunt, fub altitudine feptuaginra novem graduum, quinquaginta minutarum, hāc terram noftro jdiomate Spitfbergen dixere, ob multitudinem nivis & montium glacialium altitudinem. Hinc latus Occidentale hujus infulæ legerunt, ad altitudinem feptuaginta novem graduum, finum ingreffi, intra promontorium Infulæ, quam hodie Angli Principis Caroli dixere, ibi cum biduum hæfiffent, enavigarunt ad promontorium boreale, quod Angli in tabulis fuis appellant Faire Foorlant, noftri vero ob copiam avium, quæ in vela incidebant, dixere idiomate noftro Vogelhoeck : legerunt ita littus Auftrale, glacies enim erat impedimento, quo minus mare altum peterent, ut patet ex eorum editis libellis : In hac infulâ non ita intenfum effe frigus jndicabāt ut in Novâ Zemlâ, campos fe vidiffe virenteis, hinnulos, Anferes minores quamplurimos, ovis incubantes, cum

dicantur

dicantur in Scotiâ in arboribus nafci. Invenerũt ibidem dentes Morfarum, etiam cadaver Balenæ, mari innatans: Noftros fecuti funt Angli, qui eam Infulam luftrarũt, ut pinguedinem marinarum belluarum fibi compararent, quarum ibi copiâ maxima; Mercatores noftrates cum intellexiffent de lucro ab Anglis jam confecuto, ex arvina ifta, aut barbis balenarum, & dentibus Morfarum, qui majores pretij funt quam Elephantûm, anno millefimo & duodecimo, eò etiam naves emifere, exiguo tamen cum lucro reverfæ, nihilominus idem fequenti anno decimo tertio præftitum.

Huic noftræ fortunæ invidebant tamen Ruffiæ navigationis Præfecti in Angliâ Londini, qui naves aliquot, & cum ijs Navem præfidiariam Tigrim dictam emifere cum Præfecto Benjamino Iofephi filio, ut ōnes reliquas nationes ab oris iftis fugaret, quod & ab ipfis præftitum eft: Sexdecimenim ant feptēdecim naves noftratiũ ipfis diripuere, prædātes pro more eft quicquid ufui effe poffet, infuper iufferunt fatis imperiofe domum reverti, fub pæna fufpēdij, fi diutius iftic hærerent, non fine authoritate mandati Regij, ut patri fuo Prætori noftro, Filius Sem à Does nunciavit, quod & vidiffe fe ait: Hic filius Prætoris, cum Nauarcho Thomâ Bonaert, cũ quo hinc folverat, detinetur in vinclis, id Navi præfidiariâ Angli hujus, qui fibi in mandatis datum afferit, ut omnes Anglos, quos in navibus Celtiberorum, Gallorum, ant Batavorum deprehenderet, in Angliam captivos duceret, hæc vera effe, fidem faciunt teftes oculati reduces, etiam litteræ Nauarchi Thomæ Bonaert, & Semmij, cujus hæc verba, fub finem, in literis ad patrem, de qualitate hujus regionis.

Hæc peſima & frigidiſsima est regio mundi, undique rupes, montes, lapides, tanta ibi aquarum terram inundantium copia, ut vestigia hominum non admittat, maxima glaciei ibi copiâ, tantaq. montium glacialium multitudo, ut ab ipfâ Nativitate Chrifti concreviſſe videantur: tanta etiam nivium abundantia, ut fidem fuperet. Cervis abundat, & Vrſi & vulpibus, cervi plane funt albi coloris,

coloris, Admiror tantos Cervorum greges, unde vivant, cum regiò nivibus, tegatur, & planè fit ſterilis. Avibus luxuriant, maxime Anſeribus minoribus, qui turmatim conveniunt.

Angli profecto gaudebunt hac navigatione, maximè cum noſtros ſpoliarint, & ipſi ut Semmius refert jam triginta ſex balenas ceperant, eâ in parte Inſulæ, nec reliquæ Naves muneri ſuo defuerunt, cum binas arvinâ onuſtas domum miſerant, ipſæ pænè ſint onuſtæ. Hippopotami ipſis nullo loco ſunt, cum nullus ex ijs fructus, noſtri ijs gaudent, paucos tamē cepere Navi quadam, quæ piratarum Anglorum manus evaſit. Fortaſſe ſequenti anno noſtrates Mercatores periculum facient armis, an penes noſtrates ſit ibi ius piſcandi, qui primum deteximus, ut apparet ex hiſtoria de Ioanne Cornelij Rijp, an penes Anglos, qui primum piſcati ſunt : quod faxit Deus, in patriæ noſtræ commodum.

De omnibus Septentrionalium regionum ſitubus, in frotè tabellum quandam adieci, exactè delineatam, quà ſtudioſè deſignaui ſingula, quæ in oris hiſce ſunt detecta, ut vero omnibus curioſis ſatiſſacerem, veram ſubjunxi formā, Morſarum, quas nos VValruſſos, Angli Zeehors appellant. Species eſt Cuniculorum aut Canum marinorum, magnitudine boves ſuperantes, pellis ad nos allata quadringentas libras pendebat.

F I N I S.

Veram effigiem Balenarum exhibemus, quarum offa, & pingue-
do maximo funt ufui, funt & aliæ, eiufdem generis, fine barbis, ex
quibus nullum oleum conficitur, ita viribus valentes, ut fcaphas in
mare demergant, ab ijs, hæ difcernendæ, quod in dorfo pinnis care-
ant, illis vero in cavitate intra nares & caput, fi capere velis, har-
pagones infigendi funt, aut poft ipfas pinnas, quas in latere poft ca-
put habent, hæ fæpè longitudinem feptuaginta, aut ostoginta pedum
fuperant.

*Vm temere, & inconsideratè antea scripserim, hosce mercatores nostros sequēti anno cum Anglis bello certaturos, ac de libertate piscationis apud Insulam Spitsbergensem cum ijsdem dimicaturos; Ab ijsdem mercato-*ribus, ejusdem navigationis autoribus, satis acriter sum reprehensus, qui nequaquam contra serenissimam Magnæ Britanniæ Majestatem, se opposituros declarant, ut pote quam in magno habeant, respectu, atq; (qua par est) reverentia; quod quidem prudenter ab ijs factitatum esse judico, propterea quod, summopere confidant, quod audita & intellecta eorum causa atq; querela, eos, ut subditos ordinum sibi religione & fædere junctorum, secundum magnam humanitatem suam Rex Britanniæ sit protecturus, adversus vim (à Capitaneis suis, sub ejus titulo & prætextu) hac æstate navibus nostris illatam, similiterq; mandatarus restitutionem rerum nobis jam pridem ereptarum. Quod si ne hoc quidem adhuc mandaretur, atq; a Maiestate sua injungeretur, constituerunt tamē æquo animo ferre, quicquid a dicta Majestate in hoc negotio ordinatum fuerit, neq; ullo modo arma adversus eam movere, quibus se effecturos esse non sine causa autumant.

Vt tamen de jure eorum satis evidenter omnibus pateat, sequentia quidem his adjūgere consultum putavimus, quæ quidem à doctiss. Cosmographo Petro Plancio secundum rei æquitatem atq; mensuram conscripta sunt.

G

Refutatio rationum, quibus Angli Dominationem Piſcationis ad Inſulam Spitſbergenſem ſive Novam Terram prætendere & defendere conantur.

 Ui Anglicanæ Navigationis cognitionem habēt non ignorant, quam iniquis rationibus nitantur, & defendere conentur Angli, Equitem Hugonem Willougby (Capitaneum trium navium, Vocatarum, Bona Eſperanza, Eduardus Bona adventurus, & Bona Confidentia) inveniſſe & detegiſſe magnam illam Inſulam Spitſbergenſem, idq; ſeptimo anno Regni Eduardi ſexti, anno nimirum Domini 1553. Nam eorum rerum maritimarum ipſæ lucubrationes atq; ſcripta, contrarium manifeſtò teſtantur, nimirum prædictum Equitem cum tribus iſtis navibus ex portu Anglicano Ratcliff ſolviſſe, (ut Septētrionē verſus Regnum Cathaya detegeret) 10. May 1553, & ab Inſula Norvegiæ Seynā 30 Iulij; Eumq; duabus navibus, matutino tempore 14. Auguſti, terram quandam detegiſſe ſitam à dicta Inſula Seynam (Meſocæcias) 160. Anglicanis Leucis (milliaribus nimirum Germanicis 120.) ad altitudinem 72. graduum: Quod quidem præfatus Eques propriâ manu Anglicè conſcripſit his verbis.

The 14. day earely in the morning we deſcovered land, wich land we hare with al, hoiſing out our boat, to déſcover whath land it might be, but the boat could not come to land, the water was ſo ſhoare, were was very much yſe alſo, but there was no ſimilitude of habitation, and this land lyeth frō Seynam 160. leagues, being in latitude 72. degreas, then we plyed to the northward the 15, 16, and 17. day.

Hoc eſt

Decimo quarto die mane, terram quandam detegebamus, eâq; omnino & viſibiliter detectâ, ſchapham noſtram in mare deduximus, ad inveſtigandam qualitatem iſtius terræ, ſchapha vero ad littus pertingere nequibat, propter aquæ penuriam & glaciei ibi exiſtentis copiam; nulla vero ibi habitationis ſimilitudo; & hæc quidem

dem terra ab Infula Seynā diftat 160. Anglicanis Leucis, ad altitudinem 72. grad. & tunc quidem Septentrionem verfus curfum navigationis noftræ inftituebamus 15. 16. & 17. die.

Quam affinitatem autem habet hæc terra (ab Infula Seynā, 120. milliaribus fitā Mefocæcias ad Poli elevationem 72. grad. cum magna Infula Spitfbergenfi? cum hæc fita fit ab Infula Seynā ad Hypertrafcias, ad altitudinem 72. ad 82. gradus, & ultra; cum adhuc ignotum fit & lateat, quam ulterius Septentrionem verfus fe extendat. Itaq; Infula dicti Hugonis VVillougby, & Spitfbergen, fita & pofitione magis differunt, quā ipfa Anglia, & Germania noftra Inferior. Quapropter illud, quod ab Anglis in hac caufa allegatum eft, plane eft frivolum, neque ulla omnino nitens ratione aut fundamento; eodemque fundamēto nititur hoc quoque eorum axioma, nudum nimirum vifum cujufvis terræ, ejufdem proprietatem atque Dominium evidenter detectori dare.

Manifeftum quidem, & veritati confentaneum eft Thalaffos, nautafque noftros ad lorum iftum 72. grad. nullam quidē terram repperiffe; fed cum pateat ex Anglicano Diario præfatum Equitem, Occidentalem atque Orientalem acus pixidis nauticæ Inflexionem, non obfervaffe, itaque ulterius Septentrionem verfus fuæ navigationis curfum inftituit, quam ipfe putavit: ita, ut veritati confentaneum fit, eum detegiffe atque reperiffe octo iftas parvas Infulas fibi invicem pene contiguas, ad altitudinem 73. grad. & quafdā munitas fitas, quas noftræ navigationis præfecti VVillebrordi Infulas nuncupant; ad cujus longitudinem atque latitudinē Infula VVillougby Ponitur in tabulis Londini confectis ad ufum Mofcoviam & Spitfbergam verfus navigantium; atqua ita ipfæmet eorum tabulæ rationes eorum fatis evidenter refutant.

Scribunt quoque Angli prædictum equitem cum duabus navibus in Lapponia hiemantē in Fluvio VVarfina cum focijs fuis, à vehementi frigore interemptum effe; tertiamque navem, cum Capitaneo Richardo Chanceler Mare album ingreffam effe.

Itaque luce meridiana clarius eft, Infulam Spitfbergenfem omnibus fuiffe incognitam, atque prius à Iacobo Heemfkerck,

VVil

VVilhelmo Bernardi, & Ioanne Cornelij, (aufpicio & fumptibus Civitatis Amftelodamēfis Magiftratus) eam effe detectam 19. Iunij, Anno 1596.

Cuivis & illud notum eft, quam abfurde & contra veritatem, Angli Infulam Spitfbergenfem Groenlandiam nominent, cum eæ regiones multo longius & maiori fpacio inter fe diftent, quam Norvegia ab ipfa Scotia, interlibente nimirum fpatiofo Oceano.

Quod ad fecundum Anglorum argumentum attinet, nimirū omnes Infulas Septentrionem verfus fitas Regis fui effe proprias, tam detectas fcilicet quam adhuc detegendas, hoc omnino abfurdum eft, neque refutatione dignum, præcipue vero refpectu hujus Infulæ Spitfbergenfis, cum ea, neque fitu, neque vicinitate Angliam concernet, neque ab Anglis prius reperta fit. Nam cur Infulæ Fero, Yflandia, Friflandia igitur Majeftatis fuæ propriæ non funt? cur non Groenlandia? cum eæ longè Brittanniæ viciniores fint? Efto autem Terram Firmam, Infulamve alicui effe propriā, an ideo fequeretur, navigationem & pifcationem, (fecundum Ius naturale & omnium Nationum) cuivis non patere? Hac ratione Galli neque eorum Reges, unquam pifcationem ad novam Franciam vel Terram novā nemini interdixerunt, nō obftante quod eas regiones primo Anno 1504. prius detegiffent, ibique pifcati fuiffent. Ob quas quidem rationes fperandum, firmiterque credendum eft, Britanniæ regem (qui jure optimo deum timere juftitiamque colere tenetur) fubditis fuis expreffe mandaturum, ne pofthac naves noftras magis infeftent, oppugnent vel obturbent & fecundum Iuftitiæ normam, illatum damnum cū omni æquitate reparent & refarciant.

FINIS.

DESCRIPTION

OF THE

Land of the Samoyeds

in TARTARY,

RECENTLY BROUGHT UNDER THE DOMINION OF THE MUSCOVITES.
TRANSLATED FROM THE RUSSIAN LANGUAGE IN THE YEAR 1609.

WITH AN ACCOUNT

OF THE SEARCH AFTER AND DISCOVERY OF THE NEW PASSAGE OR
STRAIT IN THE NORTH WEST TO THE EMPIRES OF
CHINA & CATHAY;

AND

A MEMORIAL

PRESENTED TO THE

KING OF SPAIN

CONCERNING THE DISCOVERY AND SITUATION OF THE LAND CALLED

Australia Incognita.

Translated from the Dutch edition printed at Amsterdam, 1612.

BY

F. J. MILLARD.

AMSTERDAM,
FREDERIK MULLER.
1875.

TO THE READER.

The appearances or symptoms of gain & profit have always excited mankind to visit unknown lands and nations. So the handsome furs (with which we are provided by the Russian merchants), have awakened in our tradesmen a desire to travel through their countries unknown to us, in which they were afsisted in some measure by a travel from the Moscow to Colmogro, described by the Russians and thence on Petzora where the nations received the Christian faith in the year 1518, and further to the Oby, and still a little further onward, in which innumerable fables have been mixed up of Slatababa, the golden old woman with her children, and the monstruous people beyond the Oby. This Rufsian description is of Sigismund of Herberstayn, Orator to the Emperor Maximilian, in his books on the Muscovite lands, translated and published by him. Afterwards Antonis Wied constructed a map of Rufsia by the instruction of a Ioannes Latzky, formerly one of the Muscovite Princes, who, on account of the disturbances, after the decease of Ioannes Basilius, the Grand Duke in Muscovy, had fled into Poland, which map was presented to a certain J. Coper, Counseller of Dantzich, and edited in Rufsian and Latin characters, in the Wilda, in the year 1555. Then another map of this Rufsian land was made by the English, who had traded in these quarters. These maps and descriptions, such as they are and the further knowledge spread by and by, induced Olivier Brunel, born in Brufsels, to sail thither in a small vefsel from Enchuysen; he roamed about hither and thither in the vicinity and amassed in the Petzora much wealth, consisting of furs, Rufsian glafs and crystal de Montagne, which with the boat were lost in the river Petzora. Thereupon, the former expeditions of the English, and of Olivier Brunel who had likewise been in Costinsarck on Nova Sembla, having raised in our Dutchmen a desire of gain, and enticed them by the riches of China and Cathay, to which they hoped to find accefs along these coasts, the Right Honorable States of the United Provinces dispatched thither two vefsels, that were to go with Jan Huyghen of Linschoten to Waygats, and two others with Willem Barentsz., that were directed through the inducement of Rev. Petrus Plancius to proceed to the North and sail round above Nova Sembla. But Willem Barentsz. being locked up between the land and the ice, at the longitude of 77 degrees near the islands of Orange, returned on the first day of August, and Jan Huyghen sailed quite through the strait of Waygats, and fifty miles further; but on account of the north-east wind, and the year being far spent, came back also. Both sailed out again the next year in 1595, intending to place their marks further, or to find the pafsage quite through; but the cold and ice debarring their progrefs, they could not effectuate their purpose, for they could not pafs the Waygats. And Willem Barentsz., who got a little further on his third expedition in the year 1596 than he could get on his first undertaking, left his vefsel there on the ice-berghs for a mark and perpetual memorial of the extreme sailing in the North, whose adventurous history, sad end and the crews wonderful return homeward, one may read in their printed journals.

In order then, to promote in some measure, the knowledge of the locality of these lands (which our merchants
have acquired by these previous voyages), we now place in
your hands an account of the new dominion of the Rufsians
in the lands of Tartary, whence may be seen the agreement
with the very interesting drawings of Jan Huyghen, and the
further situation of the countries lying on yonder side the
river Oby.

Besides this description of Siberia and the most northerly
part of Tartary, we likewise hand you a map, translated
from the Rufsian, of all the adjoining countries, deline-
ating the entire sea to the east of Waygats, and a way to
proceed to the south of Cathay. But if the pafsage were
situated too far to the north (as it appears from the map), it
might, to judge from appearances, have been possible to get
by water to the Oby, or any other of the large rivers, for
those coasts are indeed always navigated by the Rufsians
with their canoes or small vefsels, and then they proceed
inland with boats by water or by land, and it seems one
might then discover remarkable things. But as the Waygats
is only open or unthawed for a short time in summer, as appears from the two expeditions made thither by J. Huygen
and W. Barentsz, this exploration could not easily be made,
for it appears that nature has placed the cold and the ice
there as our enemies to moderate our desires; — yet notwithstanding all the examples of such excellent men as W. Barentsz,
J. Heemskerk & J. Huyghen and the unlucky voyage which
Kerckhoven performed for Isaac Le Maire, still some inexpe-
rienced recklefs men have boldly dared to request the Noble
Lords of the Admiralty, and the Mighty Lords the States,
again to appoint them to sail to the north-east above Nova
Zembla, confidently affirming it to be, at the height of 72

degrees north warmer and warmer, on account of the long days. This was also done by a certain Heliseus Röslin, a doctor of Hanau, at the end of his little pamphlet (written and dedicated to the Mighty Lords the States in 1610, on the 22 of December,) in which (after many absurdities which he grounds on the maps drawn of Tartary from very old times, when the Rufsians themselves were unacquainted with it) he says: that the nearer the pole the warmer it is in summer time, and that no impediment could befall the vefsels on account of the ice or cold. And our people thought even that the sun would rather make salt than ice at the North of Nova Sembla. With these opinions they sailed out in the spring of 1611 to go far round above Nova Sembla, and thence, as their maps showed, to proceed south-south-east to the strait of Anian, and further to the long sought-for Cathay and China; but it did not come so far, that they could see whether their maps were correct or defective, for as they sailed out too early in the season, and against their expectation were prevented by the ice, they came to Costinsarck near Nova Sembla, and having suffered damage by the ice they ran into Moscovia for repairs. Thence, without making any further attempts, they sailed to the coasts of Canada between Virginia and Terra Nova, to take up winter-quarters, having visited nearly all the coasts to the Norenbega, where one of their companions and six others were shot with arrows. Of this company one of the vefsels came home, and the other proceeded again to the North, the better to carry out their purpose. But as the English after these aforesaid expeditions of W. Barentsz., had still made several voyages by way of trial in the north-east, the Gentlemen Directors of the East India-Company sent thither some years ago a certain Mr. Hudson, who as he could find no way in the east, sailed towards the west, whence without having obtained any advantage, he arrived in England. Afterwards, when the English again sent him out, he had much more prosperity but lefs good luck, for having after much trouble arrived about 300 miles to the west of Terra de Baccalaos, and having taken up his winter-quarters there and wishing at 52° of latitude to push on further, he was, with all the Commanders, put on shore by the crew, who refused to go further and returned home. His designs we subjoin at the close of the book, hoping that we shall receive of the vefsels now expedited thither, further news and tidings of a thorough pafsage, by which they would reap eternal honor and fame, because so many years such august personages and intelligent pilots have endeavoured to come by means of a new short road to the riches of Cathay, China, the Molucks and the Peruvian nations. Among these have been Martin Forbisher and Iohn Davis, who in the years 1585, 86 and 87 sailed between Terra Nova and Greenland northwards up to 72 degrees, but were kept back by the ice, and without having done any-thing subservient to their purpose, returned home.

The hope of finding out this newly discovered pafsage or strait above Terra Nova discovered by Mr. Hudson, is strengthened by the testimony of the Virginians and Flori-dians, who confidently affirm that to the north-west of their country is a large sea, saying that they have seen vefsels there like those of the English. We read also in Iosephus d'Acosta in the 12th chapter of the 3d book, about the natural productions of the West-Indies, that the Spaniards believe the English Captain Thomas Candish to have been well acquain-ted with this pafsage. It is also said, that the Spaniards en-deavour to keep this road unknown, and that some of them, on returning from the conquest of the Philippines, have come back home along this road. Therefore the King Philip ordered a strong fort to be built on the northern coast of Mar Vermejo, to the west of New Grenada, to prevent our nation or any of his enemies from depriving him, through this avenue, of the riches he pofsefses in peace near Mar del Zur; this has been related to us as quite true.

This road then, if it continues as it appears, will afford our people accefs, not only to the Chinese, the Molucks, or Peru; but likewise enable them to go and see what nations live on the south side of the South Sea, what harbours and merchandises are to be found there; as they will find every where plentiful refreshments, whether they go to the islands, whither the Bishop of Quito went (of which we have got information from one of our countrymen who has been there with said Bishop, and related a good deal about it to the Advocate Barneveld and the Honorable Lords Directors of the East-India-Company), or whether they land on the continent, whereof I now hand you a discourse and narrative, hoping that this may be agreeable to all those who traffic in the remote parts of the earth, and also to all who like to know more and more of the globe and its inhabitants; which knowledge I hope may increase in you to perfection and bring you riches and unperishable honour.

Your very zealous Servant
HESSEL GERRITSZ FROM ASSUM,
Lover of Geography.

COPY

There dwells a nation in Muscovy called the children of Aniconij and they are of farmer-descent, sprung from a countryman named Anica. This Anica being rich in land, lived near a river called Witsogda, wich runs into the river Duyna, that falls at 100 miles' distance thence into the White Sea near Michael Archangel a castle thus denominated.

This Anica then being rich as related, had also many children and was well provided for by God with every good thing and abundantly blessed. Actuated however by a great desire of gain, he wished to know what kind of countries the people possessed that came yearly to Muscovy to trade in precious furs and many other goods, that were òf strange speech, garb and religion and manners, calling themselves Samoyeds and also by many other names. These came every year down the river Witsogda, with their merchandises, dealing with the Russians and Muscovites in the cities of Osoyl and Vstinga on the Duyna which was, at that time, the staple of all kinds of things and also of furs. This Anica then (as just stated) was desirous to know whence they came and where they dwelt. Thinking too that great riches might thence be obtained, considering the handsome furs they imported every year, produced such

great treasures, he silently contracted an alliance and friendship with some of these peoples. He sent also some of his
slaves and servants thither, to the number of 10 or 12 along
with them into the country, ordering them diligently to spy
out every thing in the lands they travelled through and to
take due note of their manners, abodes, mode of living
and mien, and thus to give him a good account of every
thing when they came home. They having duly followed
up his orders, he treated well those who had been there and
showed them great favour, but told them to keep every thing
quite secret and made them stay with him without acquain-
ting any one about the matter. But the next year he sent
larger parties thither and also some of his friends with goods
of small value, as German haberdashery, bells and similar
articles. These men also accompanied the others and like
them pried and looked into every thing, and proceeded as far
as the river Oby through many deserts and along several of
the many rivers, contracting with many Samoyeds close friendship and alliance. They heard too that the furs there were of
small value and that riches were to be got there. They saw
also that they dwelt not in cities, but lived in companies
peaceably together and were governed by the oldest among
them; in their diet they were very uncleanly and subsisted
of the game they caught, unacquainted with corn or bread.
They were mostly good archers and their bows were made of
tough wood and some (arrows) were pointed with sharpened
stone and some with sharp fish-bones, with which they shot
the game that was found there in great abundance. They also
used fish-bones to sew with, taking the sinews of small animals, instead of thread, and thus joined the skins together
with which they covered themselves, wearing in summer
the fur outside, and in the winter inside. They likewise co-

vered their houses with elks' hides and skins which were held by them in slight estimation. In short, they examined every thing, and returned with rich furs explaining every thing to Anica that he wished to know. He then carried on a trade for several years with some of his friends, so that these Aniconij became very powerful and bought every where much land, so that people were very greatly astonished at seeing such a profusion of wealth, not knowing whence it came. In some of their villages they like wise built churches, yea, afterwards erected a fine temple in the city of Osoyl, situated on the river Witsogda, in which they lived; which temple was raised from the ground and built of clear white free stone. In short, they knew not what to do with all their goods.

They now wisely perceived that their good luck might at one time be reversed, as often happens in such cases, seeing that they were every where much envied by strangers on account of their riches, though they never offended any one, and endeavoured with great caution not to do so in order to retain the same position they held. According to the Muscovite customs they generally say: „he that has no friends at court is like nobody", because in Muscovy whoever is endowed with any thing another has not, is envied and slandered at court, and if he has no friend, is without any right or reason oppressed, yea trodden under foot. They therefore, being rich, had already a friend, who was held to be one of the first, and he was named Boris Goddenoof and brother-in-law to the Emperor Fedor Ivanowitz, who then reigned, and Boris was after the emperor's death chosen in his stead Russian Emperor, as is more fully related in the late description of the Muscovite wars.

So they resolved then fully to reveal every thing unto Boris, first offering him some presents, as one is accustomed to do, and requesting him to give them a hearing, as they wished to make known unto him a matter which would profit the whole realm. Boris readily listened to them and showed them much more kindneſs than before. When they had related every thing unto him about the researches they had made with respect to the Samoyed and Siberian lands, and also what they had observed and seen there and described what wealth might accrue to the country, they only did not reveal to him in what clandestine manner they had acted, nor told him either how rich they had first made themselves: this they said nothing about. And now Boris began to burn with desire and wished to examine all this; yea, he loved them as his own children and greatly extolled them giving them letters of credence in the Emperor's name, that they might without contradiction, eternally, and by right of bequest occupy their lands according to their free will and good pleasure, without any tribute now or for evermore. He likewise had them conveyed in his own sledge when they were in the winter in Moscow, this being held a great favour among the Moscovites and chiefly when shewn them by such a mighty prince as Boris was, one who reigned supreme throughout the whole empire.

Boris having duly considered this, discovered all to the Emperor, to whom the news was most agreeable, and who honored him now the more for it, and allowed him to act in this matter as he pleased. Boris, without delay, engaged some captains and poor noblemen towards whom he felt favourably disposed, ordering them to depart with those whom the Aniconij would give them, and to equip them in costly garments as ambassadors, adding, besides, some soldiers and also gifts of small value to give to the nations whom they were to visit. He ordered them to note down all paſsages, rivers, woods and places; also their names that they might be able to give a satisfactory account of the same, when they should return. Furthermore, he enjoined them to act amicably, to observe a pleasant deportment towards the nations, to spy out some convenient locality, suitable afterwards for the erection of strongholds and castles, and to get some of the people introduced into Moscow, if in any way poſsible. In this manner they left Moscow, provided with clothes, guns and ammunition and also presents, and then came to Witsogda, to the Aniconij, who induced people to go with them; also many children and friends of theirs accompanied them thither.

Having arrived there, they did what was told them, and showed the people great friendship, enquiring diligently who were the most distinguished among them, upon whom they conferred great honour, giving them many presents of small value, which however seemed in their eyes to be very precious and costly: — yea, they awaited them with great rejoicing and shouting, falling down at the feet of the givers, seeing them dreſsed in such costly raiments, and not being accustomed to this they thought them Gods.

But when the Muscovites spoke to men conversant in the languages, who were Samoyeds and who had dwelt for some years with the Muscovite farmers in villages, and had learned the language, they told them their Emperor was nearly a God; yea, speaking of many things, they excited in these poor people a desire to see this, who, wishing for nothing better, accepted the proposal; they asked moreover if they would leave some Muscovites· behind with them, as hostages to learn the language. So they got many of these people on this side the river Oby to take their part, who submitted to the Muscovite Emperor, and directly allowed the Muscovites to levy a tax on them. They promised, besides, to pay each of them, and even their children that had only just learned to handle a bow, — a couple of sable skins, which they considered, among themselves only, of small value; but held by the Muscovites to be like jewels and then promised to hand over these gifts to those who might be appointed to receive them, and this literally happened.

They then crofsed the river Oby and traversed the country to the extent of 200 miles, while they beheld many rare animals, beautiful fountains, fine shrubs and woods, and also a great number of Samoyeds; some of whom rode on elks and others were sitting in sledges, drawn by stags or dogs thad had the swiftnefs of stags. In a word, there were many things to excite their wonder, all of which they took good care to note down in due order, so that they might afterwards give a good account of every thing they saw. Then they returned, taking a few well disposed Samoyeds along with them, and leaving some Muscovites in the country to learn the language. Upon arriving at Moscow they brought an exact account of every thing to aforesaid Boris and Boris again informed the Emperor. With great astonishment they looked at the Samoyeds, that had come with them, who were ordered to shoot, and which they performed with such dexterity, that they could scarcely believe their eyes. For a small piece of coin, smaller than a halfpenny, they placed as a mark in a tree, and then went away from the mark at such a distance that they could scarcely see it any longer. Notwithstanding they hit the mark as often as they shot at it, to the astonishment of the beholders.

These wild people, in their turn, beheld the manner of living of the people of Moscow with great wonder, and also the customs of the city and such like things. But they were struck with awe on beholding the Emperor, decked in costly array, sitting on horseback, or riding in a coach drawn by a great number of horses splendidly equipped, and surrounded by many high dignitaries in costly apparel. They likewise gazed intently at all the soldiers who, gun in hand, walked in red coats along the train; the Emperor being always when he rode out, surrounded by four hundred guardsmen. With great astonishment they also listened to the chime of the clocks which are very numerous in Moscow. Nor did all the splendid shops and magnificent articles the lefs attract their admiration. In short, they fancied that they had got into the abode of the Gods, and wished much to be again with their brethren to relate all this to them, calling them happy who might obey such a master as the Emperor, whom they thought a God. Also the food, they received in Moscow, they liked much, discerning very well that it was of much better taste than the raw beasts or dried fish they had at home.

In short, they promised the Emperor to acknowledge him as their sovereign Lord and to persuade their fellow countrymen, far and near, to do the same. They requested the Emperor, graciously to send them governors to rule over them, to whom they would then pay the aforesaid tribute. As to their idolatry, no notice was taken of that, and they retained their old notions, but I believe that the Christian faith would soon be introduced, as soon as Christian teachers were appointed for that task; and this will be the case, if they are not so much engaged in carrying on violent wars.

All this, having thus happened as above mentioned, the children of Aniconij were highly extolled. Every where much liberty was allowed them, and they were even entrusted with the government of some places on the vicinity of their own lands, which were extensive and important. They even owned a large extent of country, hundred of miles in circumference, situated along the rivers Duyna, Witsogda and Soehna, so that they became rich and opulent and were daily loaded with honours.

In Moscow they resolved, after deliberation upon the sub-ject, to build there along and near the river Obi, in the plain field, strongholds, in spots which nature pointed out as fit localities for the purpose. These fortrefses were then to be provided with soldiers, and a general Governor appointed to extend and explore the country, and eventually to incorporate it. All this took place as aforesaid. First some castles were built, for which large beams were supplied from the neigh-bouring forests and then filled up with clay; then these strong-holds were filled with soldiers, while many people were sent thither daily, and in time, formed large communities composed of Poles, Tartars, Rufsians and other nations.

Bad people, under sentence of banishment, traitors and thieves, and the like refuse of mankind, who had deserved death, were sent thither. Some of them were kept in con-finement, and had to stay there according to the nature of their punishment. In this way, by degrees large cities and communities sprang into existence, forming now almost a kingdom, and many poor people went thither, as they enjoyed many privileges and had land for nothing. This country was called Siberia, and a city was built called Siber. When they first heard in Moscow of Siberia, criminals trembled, just as in Amsterdam malefactors were frightened at the name of the penitentiary. For such people were sent immediately to Sibirdam. It has now become so common, as to attract little notice, though the lords and nobles who have incurred the Emperors' displeasure, are still afraid of being sent thither for some time, with wife and children, to hold some office, till the Emperors' anger is turned away, when they are again ordered back to Moscow.

In order now to know the way from Moscovia thither, I will next relate to the best of my power, in as far as I have been able to acquire the means with great trouble, through the favour of some friends at court in Moscow, whom I got when I lived there, and were kindly disposed towards me and gave me the permiſsion, which they scarcely would have dared to grant, had it not been for my long entreaty. Had it become known in time of peace at Moscow, their conceſsion would have cost them their lives, for the Muscovites are such kind of people that they will not allow the secrets of their country to be divulged.

A SHORT ACCOUNT OF THE ROADS AND RIVERS FROM MUSCOVY,

EASTWARD AND EAST-TO-NORTH LANDWARD, AS IT IS ALREADY
DAILY TRAVELLED OVER BY THE MUSCOVITES. ALSO THE NAMES
OF THE CITIES BUILT THERE BY THE MUSCOVITES, WHICH
WERE TOO IN POSSESSION OF ITS GOVERNOR, WHO
ORDERED THE COUNTRY INHABITED EVERY WHERE
TO BE EXPLORED AND OCCUPIED, NEARLY AS
FAR AS GRAND TARTARY.

———————

From Witsogda Soil, where the Aniconij reside, they
travel the river upwards, till they come to a little town,
inhabited by the Muscovites, called Javinisco, at a distance
of 17 days' journey from the city Soil, up the river, travelling along rivers and through woods. This river Witsogda
falls from a range of mountains called Joegoria, which extend
from Tartary southwards, to near the Sea northward. From
the same mountains falls the river Petsiora, which throws
itself into the sea on this side of Waygats.

From Javinisco, travelling onward for the space of three
weeks, they come to a river called Ne-em or „Stom" (silent)
in Dutch, so called on account of its silent course between
the woods. Having travelled about five days in boats or
rusts this river Ne-em, they have to carry their boats for
more than a mile by land, for this Ne-em takes another
direction than the one they have to follow, so that for short-
nefs' sake they travel a mile by land. They then reach a
river, called Wyssera, and this river throws itself from rocky

cliffs, named Camena by the Muscovites, lying also in the mountains Jòegoria. Thus travelling along the river downwards for 9 days, they arrive at a small town, called Soil Camscoy, which is built by the Muscovites as a resting place for travellers, for this is a starting point to go farther by land, and the river runs on in its course, and at last falls into the river Cam. — This river flows below the city Viatea in Muscovia, and terminates in the great river Rha or Volga, which flows into the Caspian sea with 70 inlets. All this is confirmed by the testimony of persons, who have themselves seen and enquired into it.

Having stayed at Soil Camscoy, many horses were brought in course of time, and the place becomes already well-peopled and the country, round about, well-provided with villages and cattle. Being mostly Rufsians and Tartars, they place their baggage on horses and travel from there mostly over mountains covered with pines and firs, and other singular trees, and crofs a river in the mountains called Soyba and another called Coosna, both running towards the north. These mountains are divided into three parts and it is a very different country from the one they left, producing finer woods, firmer timber and also many herbs growing there. Their name during a journey of two days is Coosvinscoy-Camen; the two following days the name is Cirginscoy-Camen; and then during a journey of four days Podvinsco-Camen, and at last one arrives at a city called Vergateria. These three afore-named deserts are mostly frequented by wild Tartars and Samoyeds, who are constantly employed in catching costly game for the Muscovites. That range of mountains, Podvinscoy-Camen, is the highest and, in many places, covered with snow and clouds; it is very difficult to travel over, but it becomes by degrees very low.

On coming to afore-said Vergateria, the arrival of spring must be awaited, as there is a river Toera which is very shallow all the year round, deriving there its source, but in spring the snow of the mountains 'makes it very deep and they then travel further on by means of boats and barges.

This city Vergateria is the first in the land of Siberia and was built 21 years ago, with other cities round about, and is well peopled; they also cultivate the land as they do in Muscovy.

There is likewise a Governor, who sends every year in spring a large quantity of provisions and grains, all along these rivers throughout the Siberian land in all castles and places where soldiers and military men are. This is the case too beyond the Oby in all places and fortrefses belonging to the Muscovites, for there they do not as yet regularly cultivate the ground, the Samoyeds living on game, as has already been stated.

Sailing down this river Toera, so called, they arrive after five days at a city Japhanim, built two years ago, and supplied with inhabitants.

On reaching Japhanim, they travel on to said Toera and after two days'journey, this river begins to take a very crooked course, so that they are often obliged to set on land to keep the right direction and take the shortest way.

This place is now inhabited by Tartars and Samoyeds, who keep cattle as a means of subsistence, and have boats besides.

After proceding from the river Toera, they come to a large river Tabab, this being about 200 miles from Vergateria. Next, they reach Tinnen, a well peopled city, also built by the same afore-said. Many travel also from Japhanim in sledges during the winter, as far as Tinnen, in twelve days, and an extensive trade is now carried on in furs between the Muscovites, the Tartars and Samoyeds; and this is a very convenient place for those who want to be absent only for half a year. Many however prefer going further on, even far beyond the river Oby, as well East as South.

From Tinnen one reaches Tobolsca, the capital of the Siberian cities; there is the seat of Siberia and the supreme Viceroy of the Muscovites, and all cities must bring their annual tribute from yonder side as well as this side the Oby, which is collected and sent yearly, with an escort of Cossacks and soldiers, to Moscow; also strict justice is here administered. And all Governors in Samoyeda and Siberia must obey this Viceroy. There is also an extensive trade carried on in every article brought from Muscovy thither. Also Tartars from the south come at a great distance from Tartary, and many other nations who gradually arrive there, in proportion as the fame of the country spreads wider. This is very advantageous to the Muscovites, who have peacefully annexed it, so that they do not fear its inmates, who feel kindly disposed towards them. There are also churches every where; would to God the cruel Spaniards had obtained pofsefsion of America in such peaceful guise, instead of exercising such inhuman cruelty, then at least one might have not begrudged it them, for much more may be gained throúgh kindnefs as I have noticed, and as may be daily seen in the example of the Muscovites, rather than with cruel tyranny or brute force.

This afore-said city Tobolsca is situated on the large river Yrtys, which precipitately falls from the Sout h and flows as fast as the Danube, falling into the river Oby. It appears to derive its source from the same district as the Oby; on the other side of the city runs the afore-said river Tobol, whence the city derives its name.

Into the river Tobol a river falls which seems to descend straight from the North and from the mountains, near the sea-side, and is called by the savages Taffa. Near this same river the Muscovites have recently built a city called Pohem and stocked it with all kinds of people from the Siberian cities because there is such fine tillage-land all round about the country and fine forests full of game, of leopards, lynxes, foxes, civets, sabels and marters.

This city is situated at the distance of two weeks'journey from Tobolsca, to the north of the afore-mentioned river Yrtys, which throws itself also into the Oby, at the distance of a fortnights'journey from Tobolsca and at the mouth of this river there was formerly also built a city named Olscoygorot. This city was however cleared away by order of the Governor in Siberia, without afsigning any reason, I think it was on account of the cold, or because, according to their opinion, it was too near the sea-side, fearing that some secret attack or alteration might be made. A large extent of water supplied by the great river Oby embraces as with an arm an extensive tract of land, again falls into the Oby, and then forms a large island. On that island they built another city instead of the ruined one, calling it Zergolt, and it was situated about 50 miles higher up than the former had stood.

And when people sail from there up the river, they use very little tackle for their boats, either because there is little wind, or on account of the elevation of the country, for although the Oby is very large and wide, they pull the boats, as is done along nearly all rivers in Muscovy. Travelling from Zergolt about 200 miles upward they arrive at a castle called Norinscoy, built about 13 years ago, when the Great Governor sent men from Siberia in quest of lands fit for people to live in, and to build cities. Then they built there a castle, now occupied by some soldiers, in a pleasant healthy and warm place, very fertile and provided with fine animals and handsome birds. It is situated in the South-East and has afterwards become a community.

The people were ordered to seek in the direction of a warmer temperature and spy out the country, but at the same time to act in a friendly manner towards the inhabitants, whom they might meet or find, in order to get more people. When they proceeded landward in troops, to a distance of 400 miles, they beheld every where fine tracts of country, not inhabited and in a wild state of nature.

After travelling up the river Oby at about a distance of 200 miles, now 10 years ago, they came to a fine country which was very mild, so that there was no discomfort or inconvenience felt and scarcely any winter there. When they returned to Siberia, they were required to come to Moscow. Boris Goddenoof governed in that city, who took the matter to heart and directly ordered that the Governor should send people from Siberia to build a city there. This was done accordingly, and a fine castle was built with some other houses, so that it is now a fine city, called Toom, for they heard afterwards, that many Tartars had lived there, and it was reported those Tartars had given the city that name on account of its pleasantnefs. These Tartars had a king over them called Altijn; the city itself is often still attacked by divers tribes, scattered about there; but is now so powerful that it will in time become a small kingdom.

Between this castle Norinscox, this city Toom and Siberia, they still daily find many wandering tribes, who call themselves Ostachii, who now already also unite themselves with Muscovites, Tartars and Samoyeds in Siberia, and deal friendly towards them, some of them bringing also gold and other things. They have many kings among them, who are like the Indians, namely: the lesser ones who live in East-India, and not the greater. In short, the Muscovites have pushed on so far in those quarters that it is quite surprising.

There are also many castles and small cities between the rivers Oby and Yrtys which were built at the same time as Tobolsca, or a little after. These are now very rich, being mixed up with Muscovites, Tartars and Samoyeds, who are not savages, and these cities are called, Tara, near which place the rivers Oby and Yrtys are at ten days' distance from each other; another city is called Jorgoet, which was built about fourteen or fifteen years ago, also Besou, and Mangansoiscoy-gorad. These cities are situated up towards the south, but on the west-side of the river Oby, the inhabitants daily try to get further and further.

Here, on this side the Oby, lie the cities Tobolsca, Sibier, Beresai, and many others situated along-side several rivers, and many more are built daily. But the cities Narim and Toom lie on the other side the river Oby; here the people often use stags, and nimble dogs, which they feed with fish, and especially dried thornback which, according to their opinion, makes them particularly strong. The city Jorgoet afore-named lies in the Oby on an island.

Proceeding from Narim, upwards to the East, along the river Telt, they have also built a castle and call it Comgofscoy, and garrisoned it also with men. From this little castle and Narim, they were sent, more than seven years ago, by order of the Siberian governor with sledges and horses straight forward to the east, to seek out whether unknown people were living there. They travelled during ten weeks, right eastward through vast deserts, finding every where fine pasturages, fine trees and many rivers. Having travelled about the time mentioned they observed several huts in the fields and hordes of people gathered together, but as they had Samoyeds and Tartars as guides, who might have travelled over these ways, they were not afraid.

The people, they met, came unto them with humble behaviour and signified by the Samoyeds and Tartars, that they called themselves Tingoesy, that they dwelled along the great river, which they called Jeniscea, and said it sprung from the South-East, without knowing its source; but that it was a larger river than the Oby. The people were deformed with swellings under their throats and in their speech they thratled like turkey-cocks. Their language seemed not much to differ from that of the Samoyeds, which understood also many of their words.

The Jeniscea, being a river much larger than the Oby, has high mountains on the East, among which are some vulcanoes, which cast out brimstone. But on this side to the West, the country is plain and fertile, stored with divers plants, trees, fine flowers and many strange fruits, besides very rare fowl. This flat country is overflowed in spring by the Jeniscea about 70 leagues, in like manner, as they report unto us, as the Nile does in Egypt. Wherewith well acquainted, the Tingoesy do keep beyond the river in the mountains, untill its decrease, and they then return with all their cattle into these fertile plains. The Tingoesy, being a very gentle people, by the persuasion of the Samoyeds, without delay submitted themselves to the same Governors, which they reverenced nearly as Gods. What God these people worship, is uncertain, neither as yet can be known, the Moscovites being negligent searchers into such things.

And I am by no means surprised that Waygats is filled up so every year with ice in the North, as the large rivers Oby and Yeniscea throw forth such vast quantities of ice, and also innumerable other rivers, whose names are unknown, that cast up such immense blocks of thick ice that it can scarcely be believed.

For in spring the ice carries off entire forests, near the sea-side, by its huge strength and size; this is the cause why vast quantities of floating-wood are strewn all along the coast of Waygats. Also in the strait of Nova Zembla, the cold is intensest, and it is therefore not surprising that the ice is heaped up in its narrow passage, and freezes on and on; thus closely pressed together, it gets the thickness of 60 or at least 50 fathoms.

This was ascertained this year by men, who were again sent out in a small vefsel by Isaac le Maire, and who would gladly have had me too, but I declined the offer, for I will show that this pafsage is inaccessible and will always be so, unlefs some other course be taken.

The Muscovites also made a larger voyage along this river, but kept on in a straight easterly direction, hardly venturing to go South, and they had some of these Tingoesy with them, of whom they understood, that in the South there lived many nations that were quite strange to them, and who had also kings who often went to war with each other.

Not having then met with any one, they returned, after some days travelling, but ordered the Tingoesy to search farther on, who promised to do so, and contracted friendship and alliance with them, leaving some Muscovites, allied Samoyeds and Tartars with them, and giving them some presents. Next year the Tingoesy, on their side, sent people Eastwards, still further than they had been before, and went thither in great numbers. At last they found a large river, not quite so wide as the Jeniscea, but with as rapid a stream, and having kept along its course for some days, they saw at last some folks, whom they overtook, and captured some of them. They could not understand them; only by signs and gestures, they made out so much that thunder was often heard on the other side by their saying: *om-om;* and also a dreadful noise and rumour of human beings; they pointed to the river, saying: *Pesida,* from which the Tingoesy and Tartars concluded that they called the river so. From the words *om-óm,* the Muscovites afterwards came to the conclusion, that it must be the sound of bells; and departing, they took some of these folks with them, but all of them died on the way, either through fear or anxiety or change of air, for which the Tingoesy, Samoyeds and those who were with them, felt very sorry, for at their return they affirmed they were very robust people, with a good mien, having small eyes and flat faces, with a brown, somewhat tawny complexion.

The Muscovites, in Siberia, having heard all this of the Samoyeds, who came from the land of the Tingoesy in Siberia, were very desirous to make further research, desiring the Governor to supply them with men, who granted their request, even sending with them many soldiers, and they were ordered to examine every thing closely, and to take Tingoesy and Samoyeds and Tartars with them. So about 700 men departed, crofsed the river Oby, travelled through the country of the Samoyeds and Tingoesy beyond the large river Jeniscea, proceeding further and further onward. The Tingoesy were their guides, who ran before them, showing great skill meanwhile in catching on their road wherewith to supply the means of nourishment: birds, roes, goats and other strange animals; they also caught fish, the country being intersected with many fine rivers. So they came to the afore-said river Pesida, and raised huts along the coast and tarried there for some time, till the spring, when they wished to see the river open; and it was nearly spring when they got there. They did not venture to crofs the river for what had been told them before, and now discerned it was the sound of bells. When the wind came from the other side of the river, a noise of people and horses often struck their ear, and sometimes, but not often, they saw sails, going as they thought down-stream, and said that the sails were square, as I think they are in India. Not having met with any people on the side they were, they remained there for some time, and observed also that the river was very high in spring, which they did not care much about, because the ground was high on both sides. Their hearts felt quite delighted at the sight of the beautiful meadow-land, it being then April and May. They also saw many rare herbs, flowers, fruits, and singular trees, animals and curious birds. But as the Muscovites themselves are not inquisitive folks, they did not care much about these things, seeking only their own profit every where, for they are a rude and negligent people.

They then returned in summer travelling slowly, and it was in autumn when they arrived in Siberia, and made known every thing they had seen and heard, confirming it with an oath.

All these forenamed things having become known at court in Moscow, Boris the Emperor and all the great lords were much surprised to hear of all this, and, being excited with the greatest desire to have all this very closely examined, they intended sending next year Ambassadors, with many presents thither, who were to be accompanied by Tartars, Samoyeds and Tingoesy, to crofs the river Pesida, to examine into the state of things, and to form an alliance with the kings and peoples they might find there. They were likewise ordered to examine, inspect and note down minutely every thing, for they could not forget what they had heard of the sound of the bells. But all this did not happen, for at that time all this great trouble and inland wars had commenced in Muscovy, as may be understood from the description.

I presume this is the commencement of the kingdom of Cathaya, which borders on China and India, and the Muscovite may take care lest he run his head against the wall; but time will teach all, if they should try it afterwards.

Notwithstanding, the Governors sent out an expedition thither, during the Muscovite wars, in which many citizens voluntarily accompanied them from Siberia, and on arriving in the country of the Tingoesy, by the river Jeniscea, they nearly all performed the journey on foot, so that many who had been accustomed to live in ease, died of fatigue, and found at last verified what the others had said. Besides this, they heard sometimes the noise of people and bells, but being difsuaded by the Tingoesy, they did not venture to crofs the river. They saw flames issuing from some of the mountains, situated there, from which they brought sulphur and goldstone, so that it appears that many precious mines were found there.

The Governor of Siberia also ordered some boats to be made with covered decks, and commanded that they should set out in spring, from the river Oby to the sea, and keep along the sea-coast near the land, till they should come to the river Jeniscea, for he said that this river would at last reach the sea, ordering them to continue their voyage in this river for a few days. On the other hand the Governor sent out also men by land, directing them to remain there alongside the river, till they should discover these boats, enjoining them, if they did not find them, to return within a year. Those whom he sent out to sea were ordered to investigate all there was to be seen, and bade the Commander Luca to accompany them, whom he instructed to note down every thing, and so they departed. These men accordingly arrived at the mouth of the afore-said river, and they met each other there; as those, who had gone by land, had sent some on rafts and boats down the current of the river, who met the boats on the sea-side and found all as the Governor had told them before, namely according to his opinion. As however their Commander Luca afore-named had died, with some others of the chief men, they found it advisable to separate from each other, and each to go his own way, and so they arrived home again. On reaching Siberia, they noted down every thing, making a good report to the Governor, who sent it to the Emperor in Moscow, where this report was enclosed in the treasury in Moscow, till the wars should be ended; then it would be examined; but I suppose it was all lost, which is a great pity, for they have found in it many rare things of islands and rivers, birds and beasts, till far beyond the Jeniscea.

As a good friend of mine in Muscovy had a brother sent there, he gave me a blank map of it, as he had understood from his brother's own lips, who is no more, but who had himself been through Waygats and knew all places as far as the Oby; but what was beyond it he had only by hear-say; so that said very small map is merely a sketch relating to the sea coast. I obtained it with much trouble, for if it were discovered, it would cost that Muscovite his head, and therefore we pafs by his name in silence.

Into the great river Oby there falls also another river, which they call Taas, and which seems to come from the vicinity of the Jeniscea out of a large wood, whence also another river flows, not far from the one already named, and falls into the Jeniscea. So they can travel by water from the Oby through the meadow-land of the Samoyeds; proceeding only two miles by land, they come to a river called Torgalf, and arrive with the falling water in the Ieniscea; this is very convenient for travelling and was recently discovered by the Samoyeds and Tingoesy.

But it is a pity that the Dutch have not succeeded in getting through Waygats, and they do not know how to set about it; with vefsels they will not succeed, had they tried it a hundred times over. And if they would pry into all these lands, they should be obliged to remain there two or three years near Waygats or Pechora, where they would find good harbours and provisions. Thence they should send people in boats, as the Rufsians do, and also contract friendship with the Rufsians, who would then willingly show the way, and so all would be discovered.

Many fine places would be found out, islands and solid land; but it is to be doubted whether America near China is not connected with these three parts of the world by a strait, like that which unites Africa to Asia by the Red Sea; and this is indeed very pofsible; for who can tell whether it is open, except by what is found in some writings of the heathens, who afsert that it is separated from each other, for which they adduce many proofs.

If however it is open, the strait must be very narrow, for I had nearly said it would have been impofsible for people to get into America, because Adam was created in Asia, and we read nowhere in Holy Scripture that ships or boats existed before the deluge; besides it is well known that there is but one world and that man did not derive his origin in various places, but only in one place namely in Paradise, etc.

Now it might again be asked how people have every where got into the islands, and this happened, according to my opinion, also after the deluge. Likewise in America, there is a narrow strait, as we know, and perhaps such a narrow strait may be between Asia and America; though now-a-days some firmly maintain there is a large sea between both, more than a hundred miles in breadth.

FINIS.

ACCOUNT

OF A CERTAIN MEMORIAL PRESENTED TO HIS MAJESTY
BY THE CAPTAIN PEDRO FERNANDEZ DE QUIR CONCERNING THE
POPULATION AND DISCOVERY OF THE FOURTH PART OF THE
WORLD CALLED AUSTRALIA INCOGNITA OR UNKNOWN
AUSTRALIA, ITS GREAT RICHES AND FERTILITY,
DISCOVERED BY SAID CAPTAIN.

Sire!

I, captain Pedro Fernandez de Quir, declare that this is the
eighth request, I have presented to your Majesty, concerning
the population as it should take place in the country, which
your Majesty has ordered to be explored in the regions of
the unknown Australia. Without any resolution having been
taken with me, nor any answer or hope given assuring me
of my appointment, notwithstanding a sojourn of 14 months
at this court and having been engaged for 14 years in trans-
acting this buſineſs without salary, or any thing done to my
profit, acting only from motives of goodneſs; and I have
had to struggle with innumerable continual opposition and
travelled 20000 miles by sea and land, having spent all my
property, suffered personal destitution, and endured so many
and dreadful things, that they seem to me almost incredi-
ble, and all that not to give up a work of so much mercy
and devotion. — For which reason and for the love of God
I humbly beseech your Majesty that he may be pleased not
to allow me, after such constant labour and anxiety, after so
much perseverance and well founded efforts, to be deprived

e 1

of the fruits I so longed for and solicited, since the honour
and glory of God and your Majesty's service are so deeply
concerned in the matter, and infinite good will be the result,
which will last as long as the world stands, from hence
forth unto all eternity.

1. Concerning the extent of these recently discovered lands,
judging from what I have seen and from what the captain
Louis de Paez de Torres, Admiral under my command, has
informed your Majesty, there is good reason to conclude that
its length is as great as that of entire Europe, Asia Minor
to the Caspian Sea, with Persia and all the islands of the
Mediterranean and the great Sea, about and all round the
same provinces, England and Ireland included. This unknown part is the fourth of the whole of our globe and
so large that it can contain twice as many kingdoms and
seigniories as those your Majesty now holds as Sovereign
Lord, and this without being exposed to the neighbourhood
of the Turks, Moors or other nations, who are accustomed
to harafs and torment their neighbours.

All the lands which we have seen, lie within the torrid
zone and a portion of them are contiguous to the Equinoctial
line, having a breadth of 90° and some lefs, and if they continue as they promise to do, there will be found lands op-
posite the foot of the best of Africa, the whole of Europe
and the greater part of Asia Major.

I predict that since the lands I have seen on 15° are better
than Spain, the others, which are situated higher on, must
be relatively like an earthly Paradise.

2. In these lands is a great number of people; their complexion is white, brown, mulatto, Indian and mixed. Their
hair is either black, long and loose, or frizzled and curled
and sometimes red and very thin. This diversity is a sign

of their great intercourse and close contact, for which reason and on account of the goodnefs of the land and because they have no guns or other murderous fire-works to mafsacre each other, and as they do not work in silver-mines, and for many other reasons, it is probable that the population is very numerous. But it cannot be perceived that they are acquainted with any particular art or science, and they have no walls nor strongholds, nor king, nor law, being only a lot of bad heathens, divided into parties and not agreeing friendly among each other; their usual weapons are bows and arrows, but not poisoned, clubs, sticks, pikes, and shafts all of wood; they cover their loins, are cleanly, merry, reasonable, and very thankful as I myself have often experienced, so that there is reason to hope that, with the aid of God and kind means, they will be very manageable folks, soon satisfied, easy to teach and to please, which three things are at first very necefsary, to bring those people to such holy purposes as require the greatest zeal and earnestnefs. The houses are of wood, covered with leaves of palm-trees; they use earthern pots, have braided ropes and plaited nets; marble is wrought by them, they make flutes, drums, and spoons of varnished wood; they have their houses of prayer and burials, their gardens neatly got up, and hedged around; they make much use of pearl-shells, and make of them gouges, chisels, saws, pick-axes and large and small ornaments which they wear round their necks. The islanders have their vefsels well built and fitted out to go to foreign countries, all of which is a certain sign of the vicinity of a people of superior civilisation, and no less mark of this is their castration of swine and poultry.

3. The bread they eat they make of three sorts of roots, which are in great number, and require no labour, for they

only want baking and boiling, they are nice, wholesome
and nutritive, last long and there are some which are an ell
in length and half an ell thick; fruits are very plentiful and
very good; platanos in six sorts, large quantities of almonds
of four kinds; large obos, which is a fruit of the size and
taste of quinces; many inland nuts, oranges, and lemons
which the Indians do not eat, and other excellent and large
fruits of equally good quality which we have tasted; sugar
cane in many sorts and of large size is found in abundance
and apples too. There are likewise vast numbers of palm-
trees from which the juice Tuba may be readily extracted, of
which wine is made, vinegar, honey and whey; the palmitas
are very good; the fruit these palmtrees produce are cocoa-
nuts; when they are green they are used instead of cardos,
and the marrow is like cream; when ripe they supply food
and drink by sea and land; when old they yield oil for light,
and are used to cure wounds like balsam; when young, the
shells make very good' barrels and bottles; the inside of the
shell is used as oakum to caulk vefsels with and all sorts of
rope and tackle, and the usual kinds of string and tinder are
made of it. And, better still, of the leaves they make sails
for small vessels and fine mats and tiles, as a kind of thatch-
work to line and cover houses with, which are built on straight
and high piles; of the wood they make shelves, pikes, and
other sorts of weapons and oars, with many other useful
things for daily want. It is to be noticed that these palm-
yards are a kind of vineyards whose fruit and wine are gathered all the year round, no abundance is wanting and neither
time nor money required. The vegetables, seen there, are
cucumbers, large and many beets, green herbs and also beans.
As for meat, there are many tame pigs, like our own, poultry,
capons, partridges, ducks, turtle-doves, pigeons, wood-

doves and goats, which the other captain saw. The Indians also gave signs of cows and buffaloes. There are many fishes: hargos, pesce-reyes, lizas, soles, small salmons, meros, shad, macabis, casanes, pampanos, sardines, thornbacks, cormorants, chitas-viejas, conger-eels, pesces puercos, chapines, rubia almexas and garnet, and other sorts of which I do not recollect the name, and there must be a great many more besides, as all those mentioned were caught very near the ships.

If one attentively considers all that has been said, it will be found that there are so many and such good provisions which afford immediate enjoyment, so that even march-pane and many confectionaries are to be had, and without their being imported from abroad. — And with respect to the crew, there is besides the articles mentioned no lack of large hams, pots of butter and large pigs, with abundance of pickles and spices, many of which articles are like ours, and there are perhaps many more, so that this is a sufficient proof that the country is quite adapted to produce all other things found in Europe.

4. The riches consist of silver and pearls, which I saw myself, and gold which the other captain saw, as he tells us in his narrative; and these are the three richest sorts nature produces. — There is likewise an abundance of nutmegs, mastic, pepper, ginger, which both we saw. Cinnamon is known there and cloves probably too, considering other spices are found there, and those countries being parallel and little differing from Terrenate and Bachan. There is also stuff to make silks, pita, sugar and anise for distillery.

There is good ebony wood and innumerable kinds of wood, to build as many vessels as one might choose, with all sorts of material for sails, and three kinds of rigging, one of which like our hemp; and with the oil of cocos you can make galagala as a substitute for tar. A species of turpentine is found there too, which the Indians use to tar their piraguees, or vefsels, with. And because there are goats, and cows are known, there is probably Cordovan-leather, tan, and meat in abundance. As bees have been seen, honey and wax is probably found there too. Besides all these riches the existence of many other things is implied. Considering the site and position of the land, combined with the many good things which industry may add, as there is such an abundance of things indigenous and to foster ours, which I will import as soon as possible with all the other of the best and most useful found in Peru and New Spain, it appears that all this taken together, will make the country so rich, that it will be sufficient to supply itself and America at the same time, and to render Spain great and wealthy, in such wise as I shall point out, if I am afsisted by others to carry out my design. Concerning what has been seen with regard to the sea-coasts, I beg to observe, Sire, that from the very inmost part of the country there are such vast treasures and riches and good things to be expected, as we have only just begun to collect. The remark I have to make is, that it was my chief intention alone to seek for such a large country as I have found, and that on account of my illnefs, and other causes which I abstain from mentioning, I have not been able to see all I had wished; even every thing I had desired to look at, could not be seen in one month of which there are twelve in a year, and accordingly denote the several qualities and fruits which all the various lands produce. Furthermore the Indians of these lands must not be judged of according to our wants, tastes and desires and other considerations, but must be viewed as people who try to spend their lives in performing as little labour as pofsible,

which they do without fatiguing themselves in any thing that
we do.

5. The conveniences and comforts of life are found as great
there as ma y be expected in such a well cultivated, delightful and cool land, which is mouldy, fat and of a good sub-
stance, with loam-pits to build houses of: stones, bricks
and every thing else made of loam, and in the neighbourhood
also many rough and square marble-stones from which costly
and handsome buildings may be made. All kinds of wood
fit for every building purpose are to be found there; a beautiful site of valleys and fields, mostly intersected, and high
massive rocks; many rivulets and flowing rivers which afford
much facility to construct watermills, azenas, trapiches and
other water-works. Effenos, saltkilns and forests of reed
prove the fertility of the country, as reed is found there
of five and six palms and lefs, and the fruit in proportion;
at the end thin and hard, the rind smooth. There are such
good flints as any to be found in Madrid.

The Bay of St. Philips and Jacob is twenty miles in circumference; it is very handsome and free of accefs by day
and by night, and all round there are many inhabited villages, in which we saw at a great distance clouds of smoke
ascend by day, and much fire by night. Their harbour,
called Veracruz, or the Holy Crofs, is so spacious that
it can contain a thousand vefsels; the ground is smooth
and of black sand; there are no holes and one may fasten
anchors there at as many fathoms as one chooses, from forty
fathoms to half a fathom, between two rivers; the one as
large as the Guadalquivir in Sevilla, with breakers or high
running flood of more than two fathoms, where good friga-
tes and patasses may safely lie; in the other our barks entered
freely and drew quite clear water in all the places where it

is found. The place for the discharge of vessels runs along a shore of three miles, having for the greater part a pebbly bottom of black, small and large flinty stones, fit to ballast veſsels with. As the shore shews no signs of rents or crevices and the plants growing along the sides are green, it is evident they did not suffer from the violence of the surge, and as the trees grew up erect, without damage or injury, it appeared quite clear that there are no violent storms. This harbour, besides its spaciousneſs, poſseſses another eminent quality, namely that of recreation, for as soon as day-break commenced, the neighbouring wood resounded with the sweet harmony of many thousands of birds, among which there seemed to be nightingales, blackbirds, quails, finches, innumerable swallows, paraquitos, and a parrot we saw, besides many other kinds of birds. Even you heard the chirping of graſshoppers and crickets. All the morning and the evening many delightful odours were diffused by all kinds of flowers, even orange-blossoms and the herb alvahaca. And all these delightful things lead to the conclusion that the air must indeed be excellent there, and that nature maintained an excellent order throughout her works.

6. This harbour and bay were still improved in excellence by the neighbourhood of so many good islands, and more particularly of seven islands, of which the rumour goes that they measure two hundred miles; we know that one of them is 50 miles large, at a distance of 12 miles from the harbour.

In short, Sire, I say that on this bay and harbour, which lie 15¹/₃ degrees longitude from the North-Pole, there may be built immediately a very large and populous city, and that those who may inhabit it, will enjoy all desirable riches and conveniences which time will teach, and which may be further imparted to the provinces of Chili, Peru, Panama, Nicaragua, Guatamala, New Spain, Terrenate and the Philippines, all of which countries your Majesty reigns over, and should your Majesty become Lord and Sovereign of those I now offer, I hold them to be of such value, that, besides their being like the keys to the afore-mentioned lands, they will prove to be, according to my conviction, with respect to commerce in curious and profitable commodities (not to speak of sovereignty), like a second China, Japan and other provinces on those coasts of Asia with all its islands. To explain in short what I feel, and can prove in a meeting of geometricians, I will only afsert that these lands can supply and maintain two hundred thousand Spaniards. In short, Sire, this is the world of which Spain promises to become the centre; and please to note that for this body this is the pivot.

The mild temperature and virtue of the atmosphere is, Sire, such as may be deduced from all that has been stated, and proved by the fact, that, although our people were all strangers there, nobody has become ill, notwithstanding the usual labour, sweating, exposure to the wet, and without abstaining from drinking water, previous to taking food, or eating every thing the country produces, or avoiding the evening-air, the moon or sun, which is not sultry in day-time. After midnight a blanket was very necessary and acceptable. As the natives are in general of good stature, very devout, some very old, though they dwell very close to the ground, this is a sign of good health; for if the soil were unhealthy, they would build their houses higher from the ground, as they do in the Philippines, and in other places I have seen. So, fish and meat for instance remain sweet, unsalted, for two days and longer. — Fruit, brought from there, of which I have two specimens, are in good condition, as may be seen, though they were picked too early, because there are no sandy grounds, nor thistles, nor thorny trees, nor any growing with their roots above ground. Furthermore there are no drowned lands, no pools, nor snow on the high mountains, nor crocodiles in the rivers, nor poisonous malignant reptiles on the mountains, nor ants that are commonly very noxious in the houses and to fruit, nor niguas, nor caterpillars, nor gnats. And for this reason I maintain that this country is for our purpose one excelling all the rest and worthy to be esteemed as highly as many Indian countries, which for these very plagues are uninhabitable, also as other lands, where they are a real torment, which I myself can testify.

7. These are, Sovereign Lord, the excellencies and virtues of the lands I have discovered, of which I have taken posfesfsion in the name of your Majesty, under your royal colours, which the documents, I have about me, fully testify.

First, Sire, there has been a crofs raised and a church erected to our Lady Loretto, and twenty mafses performed in it; absolution was granted on Whitsun-day, and a solemn procession held on the day of the Holy Sacrament. In short, the Holy Sacrament, preceeded by your Majesty's Standard, made a tour through these hidden lands, rendering them herewith homage. I erected there three banners and displayed in them the two Columns figuring in your Maj. arms, so that I may say with reason, in as much as this is a part of the country, and in far as this is continent, before and behind, that here the word has been fulfilled (as the columns tell): *Plus ultra.*

And this and every thing else that was done, I have performed as a faithful subject of your Majesty's, and in order that your Majesty may immediately thereto add the glorious title of Australia of the Holy Ghost, to the greater honour of that same Lord, who has led me, shewn me the land and brought me into the presence of your Majesty, before whom I stand with the same good will I have ever felt in this cause, which I have cherished and which I am attached to beyond all measure, for its value and excellence love. I firmly believe from the wise counsel, magnanimity and christian piety of your Majesty, that the greatest care will be evinced, as indeed it should, in securing the population of these already discovered lands. For the chief reason for feeling united in this matter should be an inducement not to leave the country in a desolate and uninhabited condition, for which the only remedy is, to cause the Lord God to be known, believed in, adored and served there, where now the Devil is worshipped. Moreover this will be the door through which so many nations, now standing under the dominion of your Majesty, will receive good and welfare, and thus prevent the inevitable disasters, which would ensue, in case the enemies of the Roman church succeeded in getting there, to spread their false doctrines and thus to convert all the good, I have described, into greater evil, and call themselves Lords of India, and thus bring on it entire ruin. Furthermore I believe that your Majesty is well convinced that such ruinous consequences as I have just mentioned, and all other disasters, now awaiting or to happen in future, would cost millions of gold and many thousands of people, before it would be possible to adopt an uncertain remedy. May it please your Majesty, now you are able, with a small amount of silver, expended in Peru, to gain Heaven hereafter, an immortal name and the New world with all it promises. And since there is nobody that requires of your Majesty a menial's reward for such great and important bounties of God, now reserved for your happy times, I desire a servant's recompense, Sire, my appointment and dismiſsal, for the galleys are waiting; also I have a good deal to travel, and to get ready and arrange, while many spiritual and temporal interests are hourly involved, and can never more be recovered.

Christopher Colon, was rendered obstinate by his suspicion only — what makes me so troublesome, is what I have seen and touched and now propose. Wherefore may it please your Majesty to order that among the many remedies, only one may be awarded, that I may obtain what I desire, while I promise to be found very reasonable in all things and give entire satisfaction.

Sire, this is a work of vast importance, since the Devil himself wages such bloody warfare against it, and it beseems not that he should be found so powerful, while your Majesty is its Lord Protector.

ACCOUNT OF THE VOYAGE
Mᴿ. HUDSON.

———

Mr. Hudson, who had several times sought a paſsage West-ward, had the object in view, to get through Lumbley's inlet into Fretum Davis in a continuous sea, as we have seen in his map by Mr. Plantius, and to run westward of Nova Albion into Mar del Zur, through which an Englishman, ac-cording to the drawing of the former, had paſsed. But after much trouble he found this way, which is drawn here on this map, and which he would have continued, if the com-mon crew had not shewn so much unwillingneſs; for as they had been out already 10 months, having however been vic-tualled for only 8 months, and had seen only one man on the whole way, who brought them a large animal which they eat, which man however did not return, because he was badly treated, the common crew (when they had again reached from 52 degrees' longitude, at which height they paſsed the winter, 63 degrees' longitude, along the west-side of the bay, into which they had run, where they discove-red a full sea and high waves from the North-West), at last revolted against their masters, who desired to go further, and placed their superiors together in a sloop or boat out-side the veſsel, and then sailed with the ship to England. For this reason, when they came home, they were all thrown into prison. This summer there have again been expedited thither, by authority of the King and the Prince of Wales, vefsels to discover the pafsage further, and to search out Mr. Hudson and his friends, which vefsels are ordered to pafs both as soon as the pafsage is found, and to send home one with the tidings we expect.

Remarks on this Rufsian map, and also on the intervening passages, which Isaac Massa has added to the description.

On the map Massa has interpreted the Rufsian name, which was written in Greek letters, on the land above the street of Matseioftsar, — otherwise called Matenskinsarck and Costinsarck — by America, as he had written that in my example, which was a great mistake. For the land which William Barentsz has sailed along, and on which he built the abiding house, extends as far as even 60 miles higher North, and has always been called by the name of Nova Zembla, which means as much as New-Land, and is thought to be an island. But Ds. Peter Plantius has a contrary opinion of it, from the account of Willem Barentsz and Hans van Uffelen of Rotterdam, who have told him that they had understood from a chief of the Samoyeds on the south-side of the strait of Weygats, that aforesaid Nova Zembla is fastened eastward to the south of the continent, and that the Mar More (which he explains to be the Pacific Sea) is stopped up to the east with ice, which comes from the great rivers, and would appear also in some measure from this map, if the land which is drawn to the north of the river Peisida, and the land of Nova Zembla, were joined together.

But as Jan Huyghen writes that the Amsterdam interpreter

has understood many things wrong, and that the Rufsians have told his interpreter, François de la Dale, that no ice whatever is found ten or twenty miles through the strait of Weygats, so we leave this matter, as being as yet uncertain, in suspense. On the first place noted, of which Massa says that he will prove that one may not go through Weygats, it must be observed that he settles the matter somewhat roundly; for it had been done by the Enkhuysers, and could therefore be done again, but it is evident that it could not be done every year.

And in the second place noted, he says that it can not be done in a hundred years; however of the three times, that it has been tried by our Dutchmen, it has succeeded once. The second time they had already come to the States-island, from whence, through fear of being locked in by the ice, they returned.

And the doubts concerning the Strait of Anian, as this is generally called, he also describes somewhat loosely, for he grounds his doubt hereupon, that he does not know how the people could have got into America, if there were a wide space between the continent of Asia and America; although the Chinese and Japanese to the West, as also our nation to the East of it, have both had for long ages always vessels, with which they might easily have been transported.

This I have still to note, that I have spoken of the accident of the Amersfoort clerk on Nova Francia much too decidedly in the preface, for a matter is sometimes very different from what it at first appears, and as the causes why any thing happens are newly always unknown to us, we cannot at all positively assert such things.

F I N I S.

Printed in the United States
By Bookmasters